WORK WITH ME!

How to Make the Most of Office Support Staff

4/92

To Drew,

Best of luck
in all you do!

Bobby Bowden

WORK WITH ME!

How to Make the Most of Office Support Staff

BETSY LAZARY

MasterMedia Limited
NEW YORK

Copyright © 1988, 1990 Betsy Lazary

All rights reserved, including the right of reproduction in whole or in part in any form.

Published by MasterMedia Limited.

MASTERMEDIA and colophon are registered trademarks of MasterMedia Limited.

10 9 8 7 6 5 4 3 2 1

Library of Congress Cataloging-in-Publication Data

Lazary, Betsy.
  Work with me! : how to make the most of office support staff / Betsy Lazary.
    p.   cm.
  Rev. ed. of: Good bosses do. 1988.
  Includes index.
  ISBN 0-942361-23-7
  1. Secretaries—Recruiting. 2. Employee motivation.
3. Communication in personnel management. I. Lazary, Betsy. Good bosses do. II. Title.
HF5547.5.L36   1990
658.4'09—dc20   90-41868
                                                                           CIP

Work with Me! How to Make the Most of Office Support Staff appeared in a different form in 1988, entitled *Good Bosses Do: How to Find, Hire, and Keep a Good Secretary*, and published by AMACOM, a division of the American Management Association.

Designed by Stanley S. Drate/Folio Graphics Co., Inc.

Manufactured in the United States of America

To my husband, Carl, without whom this book could never have been written . . . and to my son, Andrew, in spite of whom this book was somehow written.

CONTENTS

INTRODUCTION ... ix

1
The Office Support Profession: Changes and Trends ... 1

2
Finding the Best Office Support Professionals ... 25

3
Building an Effective Support Staff/Manager Team ... 67

4
Communication: The Key to Teamwork ... 100

5
Keys to Support Staff Motivation and Satisfaction ... 113

6
Support Staff and the Woman Manager 142

7
Planning for the Office of the Future 153

APPENDIX 160

INDEX 165

INTRODUCTION

As a former secretary, it's exciting to see how far the office support profession has come in recent years. Advances in technology, the information age, a service-based economy and widespread downsizing have propelled support staff to the forefront of strategic planning for the office of the 1990's. The role of office support professionals is rapidly expanding. Forward-thinking companies are working hard to make the most of opportunities created by this evolution. Corporate buzzwords for the 1990's include competitiveness and teamwork—both concepts that necessarily involve the support population.

People are talking about what skills support professionals will need, as well as how managers must work with support staff, to succeed in the office of the future. There is an increasing emphasis on human resource development and training, no longer limited to the management level. Many companies have instituted training programs specifically for support staff and most at least hold some kind of educational special event during Professional Secretaries Week®. Some have included managers in support staff teamwork training. The most progressive have begun identifying career paths that include the support segment. There is even now a trade show just for office support professionals, who, it is finally acknowledged, have purchasing power and economic influence.

Work with Me! has been written to apprise the concerned manager of what everyone else is doing to fully utilize support staff in the 1990's. The book talks about changes and trends as well as attitudes surrounding changing roles. Starting with how to search for and choose the right support professional for you, you will find procedures for building and maintaining an effective support staff/manager team. You will also learn how to get the most benefit from that team relationship. Guidelines for support staff training and development are also included.

As the role of the secretary has evolved, so has accepted terminology concerning the profession. Over the past several years, I've heard hundreds of secretaries debate whether the term "secretary" has become obsolete. To complicate matters, many people confuse the word as it is used as a title for a position with its use as a label for a profession. I have always promoted the use of specific titles for positions that reflect the work done on a particular job and typically use the word "secretary" generically. To reflect changing times, you will notice that "secretary," "support staff," "office support professionals" and "assistant" are used interchangeably within this book. To help you properly position yourself on this issue, the book contains a complete discussion on titles and labels for the profession.

I thank the hundreds of secretaries and managers who have indirectly contributed to this book through their participation in seminars, workshops and special events I have conducted and participated in throughout the country over the past seven years. Friends, colleagues and fellow members of many chapters of Professional Secretaries International®, especially the New York City Chapter, are a continuing source of support, information and inspiration. I would also like to acknowledge the help and support of the following special people:

- Susan Marc Lawley, my partner in StepTakers, Specialists in Support Staff Effectiveness, Brewster, New York, and Parsippany, New Jersey.
- Susan Fenner, Manager of Education and Professional Development, Professional Secretaries International, Kansas City, Missouri.
- Jeff Slemrod, Tom Barbieri and Jean Giglio of Pfizer, Inc., New York City.
- Joan Linder of P.S. Consultants, Middletown, Ohio.
- Susan Kipp of Meredith Corporation, Des Moines, Iowa.
- Dennis Murphy of Professional Training Associates, Round Rock, Texas.

- Linda Mack of American Petrochemical Corporation, New York City.
- Jodie Berlin Morrow and Julia Woogen of Secretary & Co. and New View Productions, New York City.
- Lou Cress and Thea Tierney.

WORK WITH ME!

How to Make the Most of Office Support Staff

1 THE OFFICE SUPPORT PROFESSION: Changes and Trends

Have you noticed it's hard to find a good secretary or assistant these days? It seems almost everyone has a disaster story to share about support staff who haven't worked out and even worse ones who took their place. Overall, it seems nearly impossible to find that rare, highly qualified support professional.

You've also probably noticed an undercurrent of dissatisfaction among support staff. They want more money and recognition. They want to be taken seriously and appreciated. You may sympathize, yet feel it's not your problem. But the plight of support staff *is* your problem.

Years ago, you could get by with a secretary or assistant who was pleasant enough on the phone and who could type at a decent speed. But those days are gone. Thanks to the information age, your work pace has accelerated incredibly. You need a key person to help keep you on top of your job despite those who are doing their best to beat you out. You need someone ambitious enough to keep up with you and smart enough to master your new PC.

As a top-notch assistant becomes increasingly critical to your career success, the support staff crunch intensifies. The situation has reached a crisis point: as the growing shortage of qualified office support professionals tries to meet increasing demand, it's getting harder and harder for you to find the person you need to accomplish your goals.

INCREASED DEMAND AND GROWING SHORTAGE

Let's talk about statistics. It makes sense that support staff will be in greater demand as we move more toward a service-producing rather than goods-producing economy. The 1984–85 *Occupational Outlook Handbook* predicts that by 1995, 75% of all new jobs will be in service-producing industries. John Naisbitt envisions in his book *Megatrends* that 80% of all workers will be in information services by the year 2000. No wonder support staff are in demand—information services is their game.

The supply of qualified candidates already cannot meet the demand, and all signs indicate the problem is going to get worse before it gets better. The U.S. Bureau of Labor Statistics anticipates approximately 478,000 secretarial job openings each year through the mid-1990's. Only 5%, or about 24,000, of these openings will be new positions created by organizational growth. This leaves some 454,000 openings created annually by secretaries who retire or leave the profession for other reasons.

It is projected that *less than half* of expected annual openings will be filled by newly trained candidates entering the profession, *fewer than 20%* by graduates of postsecondary secretarial programs.* Assuming postsecondary schools turn out cream-of-the-crop, qualified novices, only 90,800 candidates will be entering the market with the kind of solid training a manager would hope to find in a new employee. That leaves 363,200 positions to be filled by candidates with minimal training—at the high school or adult education level—or no training whatsoever.

What's really scary about these statistics is that they don't even include openings created by support staff who move from one job to another. So if you lose a good secretary to a better opportunity—and believe me, there's always someone knocking on a good secretary's door with promises of a better life—you can't rely on an influx of new recruits to fill your need. Speaking of new recruits, let's look at the situation on the training end.

---

*Department of Labor, Bureau of Labor Statistics: *Occupational Outlook Handbook*, 1986/87 Edition, Bulletin 25; *Job Futures: An Occupational Outlook to 1992*, 1986/87 Edition.

What About New Recruits?

What *can* we assume about those coming into the field from postsecondary programs? Private secretarial schools and two-year colleges offering secretarial programs all have the same thing to report: enrollment is down—way down.

The State University of New York College of Technology at Alfred, New York, well respected for its office technologies program, is typical in its experience of falling enrollment. In the mid-1970's the Executive Secretarial Studies Program made up the largest student segment on campus, with an average enrollment of 180 students, about 100 of whom successfully completed the program. In 1987, there were 65 students enrolled, of whom about 40 graduated. In 1989, about 50 new students enrolled in the Department's Executive Secretarial Studies and Word Processing programs; about 35 were projected to graduate in the spring of 1990. Projected enrollment for the fall of 1990 currently stands at 30 students.

Some believe falling enrollment is partly due to there being fewer high-school-age people in general. At Alfred, it's also believed the technologies department may lose about half of the students who might otherwise enroll to an "Office Management" curriculum that doesn't require technical skills. In fact, the Chairman of Alfred's Department of Office and Reporting Technologies believes the biggest problem is that the word "secretarial" in catalog descriptions and program titles keeps students away.

Business schools and technical colleges with office-related programs are also finding it necessary to rethink the terminology used in business preparation programs. Some schools, in an attempt to attract more students, have rewritten course programs to emphasize administrative rather than traditional "secretarial" skills. For example, the Wisconsin Board of Vocational, Technical and Adult Education now focuses on technology with a new major entitled "Communications Network Specialist." They, as some other schools, have dropped the word "secretarial" from program titles, choosing instead more precise terms such as "computer information specialist," "administrative assistant/information processor," "data entry operator," "word processing specialist," "clerk typist/microcomputer," "office systems specialist." The Wisconsin Board reports that even without making significant changes in program content, the new titles have resulted in increased enrollment.

While enrollment is down, demand for graduates is high and competition for new recruits is intense. Alfred reports students graduating from the Office Management program aren't finding jobs, while graduates of the Office Technologies Department often have three or four job offers even before leaving the campus.

The Katharine Gibbs School, another well-known and respected secretarial school on the East Coast, boasts an average of *10 job offers per graduate* through its placement office. Gibbs operates 11 schools in the Boston/New York/Washington, D.C., area and reports that figure is even higher in metropolitan compared to suburban areas.

Alfred State College of Technology reports an interesting new trend in recruiting practices: the temporary agency as prospective employer. This may reflect the fact that many companies have come to rely on temporary agencies to fill their support staff needs in the common situation where they are unable to fill open positions quickly themselves. And, according to the Chairman of the Office Technologies Department at Alfred, competition among agencies for new graduates is fierce. If Agency A learns that Agency B has visited the college, Agency A will often make a second visit to try to lure students away from Agency B.

Agencies apparently are not hiring only for their own benefit, either. Alfred sees a major change in recruiting practice as large corporations sign contracts with temporary agencies to handle hiring for them as a means of cutting costs. This way, a company can try out a new secretary before deciding whether to keep him or her. This is one way to solve the growing problem of dissatisfaction among support staff. By working through a temporary agency, the company can turn back to the agency what it considers an attitude problem rather than have to deal with it on its own.

Poor attitudes among secretarial students is a common problem. Many schools report that students show very little interest in what they are learning. One school reported it was not unusual to find failing grades for students who were absent 25 or 30 times in a semester or simply stopped coming to class. An instructor at another school believes that the students don't seem to want to be secretaries—their parents put them in the school because they didn't have anything else to do. Many seem unhappy about the profession before they've even begun.

Officials at many schools claim that the caliber of students in general is not the same as it once was. Their basic skill levels, especially language and writing skills, are not up to snuff. The

Katharine Gibbs School reports that more remediation than acceleration must now be provided. Courses that were once offered as a review, such as grammar, are now the first exposure the student receives. Many faculty members believe this phenomenon is not limited to secretarial schools, but is only a part of the larger problem with education in general.

On the other side of the coin, some school officials notice a decline in the technical skill levels of incoming students. This reflects an increased emphasis on academic subjects in secondary schools that bring up educational levels, an emphasis which no longer allows the student time to focus on specialty subjects such as typing.

Alfred State College of Technology reports another trend in the student population: increasing numbers of nontraditional students. These are adult learners coming back into college programs as full-time students, often taking advantage of federal funding. During the 1989–90 school years, nontraditional students comprised 20% of the Alfred student community. Another community college reports they even have several people with Ph.D. degrees who have come back into the office technologies program because they cannot get jobs.

The fact cannot be avoided that students now moving into the support staff field are not the same as they once were. It's safe to say that high school students graduating in the top of their class are less likely to enroll in secretarial programs than in the past. Few young men at this point tend to enter what is still considered a female-dominated profession, and women are no longer limited to choosing traditionally female-dominated professions.

Other social and economic factors enter into the career decision as well. For most of this country, the days of man as provider and woman as full-time homemaker are gone. The Bureau of Labor Statistics reports that while as recently as the 1950's two-thirds of all families were of the man/breadwinner, woman/homemaker type, this is true in less than one-third of families today. The current economic climate and desired standard of living among Americans now in many cases require a two-paycheck family. Working women are no longer merely providing a secondary income. But that's precisely how many consider secretarial work—as an interim job, not a career. Support staff work is certainly currently not the first profession of choice for the serious career-minded individual.

Other social factors may influence the decision not to choose support staff work: with the 50% and higher divorce rate we live with today, women are afraid of being left to raise families and support themselves. They think a support staff career will not allow them to do so. The high cost of day care also means that it is not financially worthwhile to work as a support professional.

In any case, the secretarial-training schools are having a hard time providing what is needed by today's organization, not only in terms of quantity, but also quality. And there has been a shift in what is most sought after in a prospective secretary. While recruiters were for a while most concerned with a candidate's ability to operate automated equipment, Gibbs reports that prospective employers now consider "soft skills"—appearance, pride and professionalism—almost more important than technical skills, because practically anyone can be trained to use computers. The Wood Secretarial School of New York City echoes this experience, stating that professionalism is the key concern of recruiting corporations.

Facing the growing shortage of secretarial graduates, companies are turning more than ever to recruiting four-year college graduates who had no deliberate intention of moving into support staff work. This solution can work only if companies are prepared to meet the career advancement expectations of the '90's student. And the traditional lack of those opportunities for support staff is one reason why fewer people want to enter the profession in the first place.

Meanwhile, the office support profession is undergoing a sweeping evolution. Today's support professional is meeting new challenges, increased responsibilities, higher status and greater opportunity than ever before. It's a shame that while schools are right in step with the times, replacing typewriters with personal computers and even, at Alfred, installing computer networks right in dormitory rooms, these very schools are finding it difficult to fill their classrooms.

We need to recognize how quickly the office support profession is changing and make that fact known to students, managers and support professionals themselves in order to solve growing staffing problems. Let's talk about how things have changed.

Expanding Support Staff Roles

Advanced technology, the "information age," our service-based economy and the trend toward downsizing have resulted in swift and dramatic changes in the role of support staff. Where many had predicted the end of the secretary, or worse, the deterioration of the support staff role into that of production worker, in fact support staff are emerging as key team players with expanded roles and growing opportunities for career advancement.

Just 15 years ago, secretaries were typing letters on electric typewriters, many of which did not even have correcting ribbons. In those days, it would commonly take the better part of a morning to draft, revise and finalize a three-page letter. In the past, one of the traditional secretary's most valuable skills was correcting a typographical error inside of one minute. An even greater talent was taking paper out of the typewriter and repositioning it so that retyped corrections were unnoticeable.

Technology has allowed document production to take on lightning speed, and in the simplest of cases, freed up support staff to take on more project-oriented responsibilities. Within the last 15 years, we have moved through electronic typewriters, dedicated word processors and into personal computers with desktop publishing, spreadsheet and database capabilities. Possible job duty combinations are limited only by the latest software.

Where the secretary's job was once narrowly defined and standardized (the manager dictated a letter, memo or report; the secretary typed it up, made copies and saw to its distribution), high technology (electronic and voice mail, fax machines, computerized calendars and networking systems) has changed forever the manner in which support staff and managers work together. Also thanks to advanced technology, support staff/manager task responsibilities are often blurred. Managers with their own PC's may initiate and revise documents themselves before passing them on to their assistant. In the past, variations in the secretary's role were determined by how much a manager chose to delegate. Today, the role of support staff depends on the applications of a company's hardware and software package.

Technology has broadened the secretary's role and transformed the secretary from paper handler to true information manager. This "age of information" emphasizes the pivotal nature of the secretary's role. Where the traditional secretary filed documents into labeled folders, today's secretary is commonly involved in the research, analysis and presentation of information vital to a company's success. Support staff work has become more meaningful and challenging than ever before, and this is good news to secretaries who have long complained of being underutilized.

Downsizing has become everyday news. The trend to accomplish goals with as few employees as possible and to get the maximum contribution from every person on board has also expanded the secretary's role. As middle management positions are eliminated, tasks are often reassigned to secretaries, broadening responsibilities and expanding roles. There are as many job descriptions for support staff as there are individuals filling positions and no longer one way to describe the support professional.

Diverse Career Paths

Support staff career paths have evolved from narrow, at best, to a tree with many branches. Historically, the most a secretary might hope for was to work for higher-level managers. Opportunities for today's support professionals include the career secretary route, supervision and coordination of work, skill training and professional development, and a variety of administrative specialties, such as office management, human resources, finance management, travel coordination, customer service and meeting planning. For those who enjoy working with technology, specialties have developed, including document production, information systems, software development, research and purchasing of new equipment, and technical training. Most significantly, the barriers that once created the old saying, "Once a secretary, always a secretary," are finally breaking down. Support staff are finally being considered for promotion into other staff positions.

The Term "Secretary": Obsolete?

Sweeping changes in support staff roles and career paths have raised an important issue: has the term "secretary" become obsolete? Those who differ over use of the term "secretary" as a label for the profession seem to be about evenly divided: half stand proudly by the term and the other half strive to distance themselves from it. Some believe the word has become generic, much like the word "doctor." No one can argue, however, that the two words can be compared in terms of status. Those who stand by the "secretary" label want to reeducate everyone to a new definition of the term. Others feel it's impossible to escape the stigma attached to the word—that the perception of secretary as a dead end, limited job will forever work against people who wear the label.

Experienced secretaries argue that only true professional secretaries deserve to be called secretaries; the rest are not really secretaries at all. Newer entrants to the profession feel differently. A 1988 survey reported that 75% of 6,775 students and graduates of the Katharine Gibbs School preferred titles other than "secretary." Since it seems that people entering the profession are reluctant to be called secretaries, new generic terms are quickly becoming accepted. "Office support professionals" and "support staff" seem to be gaining the most popularity.

A related but separate issue is titles. A 1987 survey of Professional Secretaries International members reported that the use of "secretary" as a title decreased from 46% in 1979 to 33% in 1987. The titles "executive secretary" and "administrative secretary" increased in use and 54% of members surveyed had administrative titles. The National Association for Legal Secretaries also reported declined use of "secretary" as title, with 75% of members not having the title. Interestingly, the PSI survey showed that people who do have the title "secretary" have lower salaries than those with other titles. The study seemed to indicate that "secretary" tended to denote entry-level positions. In general, there appears to be a trend toward the use of more specific titles for positions that reflect the work being done by the worker.

Yes, things are looking up for office support professionals. Yet, the climate does not yet always reflect the contemporary view, as we'll now discuss.

Beyond Supply and Demand

There's still one missing piece to this story. Statistics of supply and demand are compelling, yet they don't take into account a major factor in the support staff crunch: the large number of unhappy secretaries who seek to leave their jobs.

To give you an idea of how widespread is dissatisfaction, a publication called *The Office Professional* conducted a survey in 1990 of 696 secretaries attending a secretarial convention. They found that one out of three secretaries felt that a satisfying career in support staff work was impossible under current conditions. The study related such support staff dissatisfaction to frequent turnover in their respective companies. This finding was corroborated by a 1988 study of N. E. Fried Associates which found that 31.7% of responding companies had problems attracting and 11% had difficulties in retaining secretaries. Turnover is not only disruptive and counterproductive, but costly to an organization: the Human Resource Department of Thomas J. Cook, Inc. estimates the cost of support staff turnover to average $7,600 when you consider the costs of recruiting, temporary help and training.

Many support staff professionals seek to leave the profession altogether. Evidence points to the fact that their numbers are large. The president of one secretarial recruiting firm in New York City has an eye-opening story to tell.

This agency handles strictly high-level secretarial positions, most in the $25,000 to $30,000 salary range. Linda reports that she sees a whole stratum of candidates who have no place to turn. These women (as is usually the case) are highly qualified support professionals, usually with 10 or more years' experience, often supervisory, seeking positions that are or will lead to entry-level management jobs. Such candidates don't mind using their secretarial skills. It's not that they refuse to type—they simply want more than what the typical secretarial position offers.

This group is large. Linda says at least one out of three people who contact her agency find they are really displaced. Secretarial agencies such as Linda's have difficulty placing them because such upwardly mobile support staff positions are extremely hard to come by. Management recruiting firms don't want them because their salary range is below the minimum they handle.

The reality is that entry- or middle-level management positions are filled in most organizations either by new college or MBA graduates or by promotion from within. Support staff rarely are considered for such promotions, especially those coming from the outside. Many outsiders are there for that very reason. Despite whatever education and experience the secretary may have to offer, it's the same old story: once a secretary, always a secretary.

It's not news that a lot of secretaries are unhappy. What is news is that support staff are rethinking what it means to be in this profession. The handwriting is on the wall—support staff are changing; managers must change too in order to attract and keep the highly qualified support professionals they need to get the job done.

Whenever there is change, there is disruption before a new equilibrium can be reached. What you need to get through this turbulent time is a little insight into the current state of the support profession as it affects your work life and guidelines for making the relationship work.

First, the insight. The same factors that create secretarial dissatisfaction impact on your ability to work with a secretary to your ultimate advantage. Let's closely examine this.

WHAT IS IT WITH SUPPORT STAFF TODAY?
Changing Roles and New Career Options

The feminist movement has had resounding effects on virtually all aspects of our society. Over the past two decades, broad changes in perspective and attitude have had an enormous influence on both the secretarial profession and the support staff/manager relationship. Lynn, a legal secretary for the past 15 years, is a case in point.

When Lynn was a young woman contemplating her future in the 1960's, she told her uncle, a successful young attorney, that she wanted to be a lawyer. Her uncle responded, "Oh, you don't want to be a lawyer. Women lawyers are hard and stern. You don't want to be like that. It's not suitable for a nice young woman like you."

Lynn took her uncle's remarks to heart and noticed her desire to become a lawyer didn't get much support from others either. She decided to pursue a legal secretarial career instead. At least this way she'd be in a law environment, she reasoned, a field she thought she would enjoy. A legal secretary at that time was considered to have an elite secretarial position and had a certain prestige.

How times change. Lynn certainly wouldn't get the same advice today. Young women of the 1990's are being told, "Don't be a secretary, be an executive or a lawyer"—just as they are being told, "Don't be a nurse, be a doctor" or above all, "Don't be just a housewife." The push is on for women to work outside the home and to move into more nontraditional work areas.

There is a definite pink-collar stigma to being a secretary— any kind of secretary. It affects the mind-set and behavior of those in the profession, which in turn impacts on the manager's ability to work successfully in the support staff/manager relationship.

Secretaries and managers alike have adopted an almost unconscious "just a secretary" attitude. The message is clear: It's not okay to be a secretary. Even those who are happy with their work and proud of being secretaries can't help but feel somewhat defensive. It's hard to escape the pervasive attitude that if you actually want to be a support professional, there must be something wrong with you. It's no wonder a general malaise is evident among those in the profession. It's hard to be enthusiastic when no one expects you to be.

The women's movement has stirred up things in other ways as well, as men and women, managers and support staff, search for a new protocol in working together. For one thing, classic male/female, dominant/submissive roles are no longer standard in private lives or in the office, and the helpmate or office wife role of the secretary no longer fits so comfortably, particularly where the manager is a woman.

The women's movement is the most obvious environmental influence on the support profession and support staff/manager relationship. Yet, it's only the tip of the iceberg.

Support Staff Stereotyping

The stereotyped view of the secretary as a perk of the manager's job, as an unintelligent, unambitious, less important helping hand, has created enormous barriers to manager/support staff team success. Although the secretarial role has evolved, support staff often continue to be regarded and treated as though they still functioned as the secretary of yesteryear.

Lynn's continuing saga gives a picture of what many support professionals today are up against.

After completing a two-year college program in legal secretarial science, Lynn landed her first job at a large law firm. After three months on the job, Lynn is up for her first performance review. Andrew, one of the attorneys in the department, conducts the interview.

"Lynn, we're extremely pleased with your performance so far and are very happy to have you with us. But you're so bright—you seem too smart to be a secretary. Are you sure that's what you want to be?"

Talk about a mixed message. Lynn wasn't sure whether she was being complimented or insulted. Lynn was pleased to hear she was doing so well but somehow felt guilty at the same time. She got the underlying message: Being a secretary means you're not smart. Or, if you really *are* smart, you wouldn't be a secretary.

For the time being, Lynn shrugged off the probably unintended slur because the praise made her feel worthy and especially because of the solid raise that went along with the review. She was confident that continued high performance would gain her the career advancement she desired, in terms of both more money and responsibility.

Two years later, Lynn held the same position at the law firm. A valued member of the department, Lynn obtained substantial salary increases over that time. The content of her job, however, remained the same. Despite the fact that the attorneys seemed aware of Lynn's above-average intelligence, they continued to rely most heavily on her technical skills, such as typing, filing, copying, collating. After all, isn't that what a secretary is supposed to do? Lynn craved more meat to her work, but didn't know quite how to go about taking on more responsibility.

The stereotype was at work on both sides. Lynn seemed to plug along waiting for someone else to save her from growing boredom. Andrew and his colleagues probably didn't even notice that anything was wrong with the status quo. It's a reflection of the kind of underutilization secretaries have long complained of and an example of how managers can be blindly directed by stereotype assumptions.

A 1989 survey reported in the *Office Environment Index* documented the difference between office worker attitudes and managerial perceptions of those attitudes: 82% of office employees want a challenging job, while only 52% of their managers thought that this was important to the employee. Also, 74% of support staff surveyed considered making a contribution to the company important, while only 39% of their managers thought this mattered.

Here is a summary of assumptions you must identify within yourself and abandon for your own good:

- *Secretaries lack ability.* They aren't capable of doing anything other than secretarial work.
- *Secretaries lack motivation.* They aren't *interested* in doing anything other than secretarial work.
- *Secretaries are not promotable.* They don't belong to the organizational pool of talent—they are separate and apart from the rest of the staff.

- *Secretaries aren't career-oriented.* Secretarial work is a dead end; therefore, secretaries are people who don't care about getting ahead.
- *All secretaries are equal.* Secretarial work consists largely of typing, filing and answering the telephone.

By holding to an outmoded view of the support staff role, you lose out on the immense potential of the secretary as a value-added assistant. Worse, you may well find it difficult to keep a secretary or assistant—especially that rare professional.

The "Perception Gap"

Managers cannot take total blame for managing support staff nonproductively. Traditional organizational handling of support staff also has a lot to do with the problems office support professionals and managers face today.

Most people agree that if all the support staff in an office left at lunch and didn't return, operations would come to a halt. Yet, historically, support staff have not been accepted as full-fledged members of an organization. How the support staff function is perceived compared to its actual responsibilities and the difficulty in coming up with a quantifiable measure of how support staff contribute to company goals distort their actual value to an organization. And management's treatment of support staff often reflects this perception gap.

In the past, secretaries were assigned to managers as a perk, rather than as functioning team members. While this may no longer be a usual practice, attitudes toward support staff as mere window dressing unfortunately prevail. Support staff have long been considered a separate stratum—not a part of a company's talent pool—and traditionally have received different treatment from other staff members in terms of rules, regulations and benefits.

Although they work closely with management, support staff are often treated more like blue-collar workers than the true professionals they are. Most support staff are paid hourly rather than by salary and called "nonexempt." This even sounds negative. Many secretaries, not understanding the meaning of the term, strive for promotions to exempt positions, longing to belong to the elite. They are surprised to find it means they are no longer entitled to overtime pay!

Company policies that concern support staff compensation often raise many problems. Support staff complain that although they may work late or through lunch without claiming overtime, they are allowed little, if any, flexibility in time away from the office, and may even be called to task for coming in a few minutes late in the morning.

One company found itself in serious trouble with its support staff over a policy stating that managers who worked through lunch were allowed to order something to eat at the company's expense, while secretaries who worked right alongside those managers were not. The secretaries felt as if they were not good enough to be given lunch.

It's true that federal compensation laws in some cases direct how companies must administer compensation and overtime, but not all support staff positions in question are properly classified as nonexempt. Taking into account what is actually done on the job, many support positions might well be found to fall outside these requirements. But more about what secretaries really do later. For now, the point is that whether required by law or not, these kinds of practices have a negative impact on a secretary's attitude.

One area of difficulty that cannot be blamed on higher authority is the way support staff salaries are often determined. A secretary's pay is often not commensurate with actual duties performed or the level of responsibility assumed, but rather is tied to the level of the manager to whom he or she reports. Education and experience do not necessarily lead to pay increases. And, because many organizations do not recognize a career path of the profession or otherwise distinguish among secretarial positions, salary spreads are often limited. The secretary who takes the initiative and attempts to negotiate for an appropriate salary by proving it has been earned, commonly meets with the response: "We can't give it to you, because then all the other secretaries will want it too."

Which brings us back to a misperception alluded to earlier: All secretaries are assumed equal. Organizations have traditionally considered support staff categorically, rather than individually. Little differentiation among secretarial positions in terms of titles or job descriptions is the rule rather than the exception in most organizations. At best, organizations use broad categories to distinguish groups of secretaries that share a salary level (e.g., Secretary I, Secretary II, Secretary III).

Job descriptions for support staff positions, if they exist, are often overly generic and inaccurate by failing to reflect the true depth of the position. Again, overemphasizing the typical technical aspects of the support function means little, if any, attention is given to the aspects of a secretary's position in the department and with the manager(s) with whom he or she works. It's no wonder support staff feel overlooked and less important.

Even by focusing on the technical aspects of the secretary's function, it's hard to ignore the fact that support staff positions are not all alike. Word processing and computers are utilized in different companies in diverse configurations. Some companies use a centralized word processing center and electronic typewriters at each secretary's desk. Others work with a centralized system in conjunction with satellite equipment at each secretarial workstation so that secretaries can "communicate" with the main center. The most progressive offices install computers not only at support staff desks, but in managers' offices as well. Work is initiated directly onto the computer, allowing managers and support staff immediacy of interaction. The fact that each office configuration and, therefore, secretarial utilization is different illustrates contemporary reality: there is no one clear-cut definition of the secretary.

Office support professionals are dealt with in subtle ways that reflect outmoded assumptions. They have effectively been kept to the sidelines, expected to be seen and not heard. Support staff generally aren't kept informed of the goals and activities of the companies or departments in which they work. More often than not they are left out of staff meetings, even though what goes on behind closed doors has much to do with their daily work. Apparently, it's assumed that secretaries don't need to know, don't want to know, or, even worse, aren't capable of understanding what's going on around them. In short, support staff have long been treated as though they weren't real members of the organizational team. Being continually left out leaves support professionals feeling they are second-class citizens in their own companies.

Most people consider secretarial work a dead end. If this is true, it's only because organizations keep it that way. Many companies don't bother with career planning for support staff since such jobs are not traditionally viewed as long-term career positions. There are few clear-cut career paths for the support professional who wishes to climb from an entry-level position to more challenging assignments. Traditionally, the most a secretary can strive for is to tag along as a manager gets promoted or to move up and work for other higher level managers. Even then, such opportunities for advancement are not clearly set out; support staff positions do not, of course, appear on organization charts.

Management has been slow to recognize that support staff have more to offer than just filling interim positions. Upward mobility into nonsecretarial positions has traditionally been the exception to the rule. An invisible but definite barrier has kept support staff in their place—and this has a lot to do with dissatisfaction. The conclusion of Lynn's story is illustrative.

Three years into the job, Lynn remained content, learning all about functioning in a large organization and her particular field of law. But she craved more challenge. When a position for a paralegal opened up in the department, Lynn was very excited about it. After all, she had been around for a while and had learned a lot about the inner workings of the department, to say nothing of how the attorneys liked things done. Further, Lynn was familiar with this particular area of the law and had built up a solid knowledge of court procedures. Her two-year college education was a bonus when added to her extensive experience. She applied for the job, confident she would be the department's first choice. After all, hadn't Andrew himself said that Lynn was too smart to be just a secretary?

Well, Lynn wasn't chosen for the position. In fact, she wasn't even considered for it. She was told it was because she did not hold a bachelor's degree. It didn't make sense, though, since Lynn knew that exceptions to that rule had been made in the past.

Some time later, an attorney shared the truth with Lynn. Apparently, another secretary in the firm had been promoted to paralegal and had been unable to perform the new required duties. Management also feared that if secretaries were routinely promoted to other positions, the firm would lose all its good secretaries.

Add it up: Secretaries lack ability, secretaries are all alike, secretaries are not promotable. The result of this kind of illogical thinking causes a company to lose the valuable contributions a secretary may have to offer and also demoralizes every secretary in the organization. The knowledge that no matter how high your performance, you'll always stay in the same job fosters a "what's the use" attitude among support staff. Is it any wonder some secretaries have negative attitudes?

It may seem that many of the problems we've discussed are beyond your control as an individual manager. Later chapters will discuss these issues further and provide suggestions for how you might work around them. But for now realize that if your reply to support staff dissatisfaction is, "That's the way it is, there's nothing I can do about it," a secretary may well take your words to mean "I don't *care* to do anything about it," or, worse, "I agree with the policy." Here's where you can really run into trouble.

The Coffee Klatch Syndrome

A big obstacle to support staff/manager team success resulting directly from organizational mismanagement of support staff is worthy of discussion. I call it the coffee klatch syndrome. Support staff who feel isolated and powerless to change working conditions tend to form solid support groups among themselves. Pressure is strong within these groups to conform to unspoken standards of behavior, with the threat of being ostracized keeping members in line. And it works—if support staff are banished from their own peer group and aren't welcomed into other staff circles, where else have they to turn?

While a primary purpose of the coffee klatch is to meet the social needs of support staff, it also serves another purpose: it is the vehicle through which support staff retaliate, albeit indirectly, against management practices considered unfair and against managers who are perceived to treat secretaries in an unacceptable fashion.

The coffee klatch is often directly responsible for establishing negative norms among secretaries, not the least of which is a general uncooperative attitude toward the "enemy" (management and managers). An "us versus them" secretary versus management mind-set is fostered, and let's face it, you're "one of them"— unless you take positive steps to bridge the secretary/management gap.

Specifically, the coffee klatch influences performance standards. Behavior patterns develop, some harmless, others not so harmless, which reflect secretaries' reaction to management practices and policies. Where the secretary/management relationship in a company is healthy, this is not a problem; unfortunately, that's more an exception than the rule. Negative behaviors often reflect an attempt to take control in one situation where there is no control over another condition. Coffee klatch behaviors are obvious symptoms of serious underlying problems and those problems usually revolve around one basic flaw in the company: a lack of communication between support staff and management.

For example, it is an unspoken rule among secretaries in one company that lunch hour be stretched to at least one hour and 10 minutes. A secretary who actually returns on time at the one hour mark is frowned upon by the peer group. Within the same group, it is expected behavior in conjunction with this lunch "rule" to sign the time sheet to cover for those extra few minutes. If a secretary chooses not to go along and signs in 1:10 at 1:10 instead of 1:00 at 1:10, that secretary would cause a real problem, since then everyone returning thereafter would also have to sign in accurately. It's difficult to stand alone against the group, because the klatch holds a grudge against any secretary who refuses to go along.

This norm reflected secretarial resistance to, number one, having to sign in and out in the first place. "After all, managers don't have to sign a time sheet, why should I?" These practices also reflect the following attitudes of the support staff in the company: "Managers go to lunch whenever they please; it's more efficient if I go to lunch at the same time as my manager does. Besides, sometimes I might need to go earlier or later than just between 12:00 and 1:00. And managers stay out as long as they please. Why should I be limited to precisely one hour? After all, I often come in a few minutes early in the morning and stay a few minutes late at the end of the day. It all balances out." No one was interested in how the secretaries felt about rules concerning lunch hour, so the coffee klatch took over and substituted its own rules to compensate.

Another company went to great expense to improve efficiency of support operations and enhance working conditions of support staff and saw its efforts backfire. All new equipment was ordered—a sophisticated telephone system, state-of-the-art dictating equipment and word processing equipment for every workstation. Ironically, while the intent was to foster greater cooperation, management's actions instead served to intensify secretaries' feelings of isolation and widen the support staff/management gap.

The first problem arose when the secretaries, the very people who would utilize the equipment, were not included in the process of choosing it. They were not even given an opportunity to provide input concerning what features would be most helpful, even though it should have been obvious that the secretaries themselves had the best knowledge of what they needed to accomplish work goals.

The support staff were offended to be left out when decisions being made obviously impacted directly on their own work life. And they talked about it—to managers who would listen—but more so—since not too many managers were interested in listening—among themselves, reinforcing the group's negative attitude toward management and toward the purchases which were meant to improve working conditions, not deteriorate them.

The equipment arrived and was presented to the secretaries along with a set of policies to accompany implementation of the new office configuration. The new workstations were designed to provide continuous support coverage to managers in each department. It was directed by management that secretaries were never to leave the department unattended; if one secretary were away from the desk, another secretary had to be told in order to cover in his or her absence. Lunch hours were to be coordinated so that one secretary remained in the department at all times. The secretary who was covering the lunch period was not only responsible for answering all phones, but also for assisting any manager assigned in the department who required help during that time.

Enormous problems resulted. Not only were the secretaries resistant to the new equipment, they were resentful about the new rules they felt were "dumped" on them. Some departments simply ignored the rule concerning lunch coverage. Others followed policy only as it suited their plans, claiming unusual circumstances the rest of the time. Some of those who complied and stayed through the regular lunch hour neglected to answer the phones or refused to help a manager, replying, "I'm too busy."

More problems were created by the new policies than benefits were realized. Incredible time and energy were expended by supervisors and administrative staff in attempting to enforce policy and in constant "reminders" to support staff about correct procedures. Obviously, cooperation cannot be mandated; it must be nurtured.

Individual managers suffered the real brunt of the secretaries' resistance. Managers' phones would not be answered when they were away from their desk and often, if an emergency came up during that lunch hour, they could not find a secretary to help. If no secretaries were available in one department, a manager would run to another, only to be turned away, often rudely at that.

This brings us to the most dangerous element of the coffee klatch as concerns you, the individual manager. The group will blackball a manager who has proven himself or herself unworthy of their support. Depending on the crime, a manager can find himself completely without effective support.

Take Tom, for instance, commonly known in his company as the "boy who cried wolf." Tom is a classic workaholic. He doesn't walk down the hall; he runs. He always has more projects in the works than anyone else and, in spite of his less than graceful style, is usually successful in seeing them through to completion. He's a sort of walking whirlwind, and his office reflects it—papers everywhere, covering every horizontal surface, including much of the floor.

Tom has had difficulty keeping secretaries—he's been through three this past year. Even when there is a secretary assigned to him, he always seems to have too much work for him or her to handle. When that happens, which is frequently, Tom runs down the hall to find another secretary to help him. He always says, "Please help me—I've got this super rush and my secretary can't do it." Although it was a "rush" to Tom in that he couldn't wait to get it done, many times the project wasn't really a "rush" in the accepted meaning of that term, i.e., "must go out today." Secretaries would find that they had done something for Tom, putting their own work aside, only to find the same document sitting on his desk two days later. Word spread about Tom. It got to the point where none of the secretaries believed a word he said—in their minds, nothing of Tom's was a rush. The group decided he was "out." Not only could Tom not get help from other secretaries, he soon found that many of the in-house temporaries refused to work with him either. And this was a serious problem when his own permanent secretary resigned and it took two months to find a replacement.

The coffee klatch syndrome wreaks havoc in many a company. If upper management recognizes secretarial noncooperation as a symptom of underlying difficulties, rarely does it seek to get to the root of problem situations. Unless the doors of communication are opened, the gap between secretaries and management only widens. We'll talk more about communication in Chapter 4. For now, realize that you may well be up against a problem in your company that's bigger than both you and your secretary.

If you work in a company with a strong, negatively motivated coffee klatch, it will be up to you to develop a relationship with your secretary that will override the influence of that peer group. The good news is that what often matters most to a secretary is how he or she is treated by individual managers. As you read on, you will learn how to rise above whatever organizational ills your secretary suffers.

WHAT IT ALL MEANS TO YOU

It should be clear by now that there's a problem and the problem is yours. Statistics tell the big story. You are living the smaller picture, perhaps with a secretary who is less than satisfactory or with a terrific secretary you fear will leave you. The dread you feel about searching for a new secretary is real. It's a seller's market—secretaries have the luxury of choosing for whom they will work. It's up to you to make sure the secretary you need will choose you.

That's part one of your challenge. Part two has to do with successfully managing the support staff/manager relationship and taking best advantage of the potential of that relationship for the benefit of your own career.

Your Assistant—Your Work—Your Career

You realize that good office support makes the difference between a pleasant workday experience and a daily nightmare. But did you ever stop to think about how support staff can impact on the successful completion of your work goals and, in fact, your very career climb?

Although support staff generally have little legitimate authority within an organization, they exercise real influence in several ways. Whether your secretary or assistant will choose to act to your advantage or disadvantage depends on the overall quality of your relationship. It's important to be aware of how you are vulnerable and why it's so important to build and maintain a mutually satisfactory work relationship with your secretary.

The most obvious source of a secretary's power is control

over your work product. You must rely on support staff to hold up one end of your work responsibilities, yet your secretary or assistant alone determines how quickly work will get done and the quality of that work. And this aspect of the secretary's hold on a manager is intensified in the case of those who must share a secretary with one or more other managers.

The support professional's most significant source of power is the information he or she comes to acquire on the job. Support staff are in a position to gather and disseminate, withhold or share, a wealth of information—more information than you probably ever stopped to think about—that can bear heavily on your job and career.

Let's start with the most obvious. The secretary is usually the first to see your mail. Your secretary or assistant may also screen your phone calls. It's up to him or her how much information will be passed on or screened out before it reaches you. Information sabotage need not be malicious; some people are just not motivated enough to care whether they help or hurt a boss.

A support professional's access to information goes well beyond papers that cross a desk or words that travel over a telephone line. Because of the support staff role, and also because they are often situated out in the open in an office, they are privy to all kinds of valuable information that can benefit—or harm—a manager.

Although support staff are officially left out of the formal communication chain of an organization, they are "linking pins"—major hubs—in the informal communication network of a company. As key players in an organization's information communication chain, secretaries often hear others talking within the company about you or your department, or about matters which impact on you or your department. How support staff choose to participate in this exchange of information depends in large measure on the nature of the relationship they share with their managers. A secretary can pass information further along, or ignore what is heard. A secretary can add further information to the grapevine—perhaps your secrets or disparaging remarks—or simply choose not to correct whatever inaccuracies are heard. It all depends on how the two of you are working together.

Another source of support staff power is public relations, both inside and outside the company. A secretary represents a boss and a company on the job and off. Naturally, how support staff talk about you and your company when you're not around is of great significance. Again, how a manager and company are portrayed by a secretary depends on the person's experience on the job.

Don't underestimate the amount of influence your secretary or assistant can wield over your fate. On the up side, in the successful support staff/manager relationship, these sources of power can be put to use for your definite advantage. You can gain an important edge in climbing that ladder of success by winning your secretary or assistant over as an ally and utilizing his or her full range of talents and abilities, including the power sources we've just discussed.

Take It from Here

Essentially, today's support staff/manager experience is based on the influence of a time gone by and what the future requires. Attitudes toward the support profession and the support professional's role need to catch up with the reality of what is needed by today's manager. An enhanced image of the profession is necessary to turn the tide, and it starts with you. It's your challenge to find a secretary or assistant who meets your needs and to build a successful, mutually beneficial support staff/manager relationship despite these difficult times. The following chapters will help you do just that.

FINDING THE BEST OFFICE SUPPORT PROFESSIONALS

Just how hard is it to find a good secretary? Some might argue there really is no shortage. A head count might indicate that, technically, there are enough to go around. But we're talking about finding you a secretary or assistant who's top-notch, not just in terms of skills, but also intelligence, initiative and motivation—someone who can really help you get ahead in your career. This is where the difficulty lies, for the real support professional is in short supply, hard to find and not easily snared.

There are a lot of "secretaries" out there, for sure. The problem is that broad use of this title allows for confusion over its definition and a wide range of competency levels among those wearing the label. As the term is currently used, "secretary" can mean someone who has just finished an eight-week correspondence course as well as the seasoned professional who holds a bachelor's degree and a CPS® rating.* In practice, many who call

---

*Certified Professional Secretary®, a distinction awarded by the Institute for Certifying Secretaries, a department of Professional Secretaries International (PSI). Holders of the CPS® rating have met certain education and work experience requirements and passed a two-day, six-part examination measuring secretarial proficiency.

themselves secretaries really don't fit the bill in today's marketplace.

In spite of the professional secretary's attempts to battle long-standing stereotypes, there are many who, feeling defeated by longtime treatment as second-class corporate citizens, have bought in to the stereotype. It's this type which clings to an adversarial mind-set, reflects an unprofessional image, possesses an "it's just a job" attitude and generally does as little as possible to get by on a day-to-day basis—to the detriment of the good name of the profession.

Yes, there are more than enough gum-chewing, clock-watching, underqualified secretaries to go around—employment agencies can easily waste your time with a parade of candidates who just don't pass muster. But true career-oriented, highly motivated, competent professionals are in short supply and high demand.

So, when we talk about finding you a qualified support professional, we're not talking about a simple selection process, because selection implies a choice from among ample candidates. What you're really doing is recruiting. Your search therefore takes on an important dual marketing aspect—that of marketing you, as a desirable manager with whom to work, and of marketing the position you have to offer as one which will be attractive to the high-caliber secretary. Of course, not every top-notch secretary you encounter will be right for you. So the process also includes a screening component designed to help you choose not just a competent secretary, but the secretary who is best for you.

Using the insight you gained in Chapter 1, you can gain an edge in attracting a good assistant by positioning yourself as top contender for the title "good boss." The contemporary support professional seeks the manager who shares an enlightened view.

Highly qualified support staff will not stand for being underutilized or undervalued. The contemporary secretary wants an active, productive role for the benefit of the boss, the department and the organization—but also for the secretary's own career growth. Competent professionals resent being considered a part of the office equipment; they expect to be regarded and treated as significant members of the organizational team.

Abandon any worn-out notions you hold and adopt a progressive set of beliefs concerning the secretary:

- A secretary is an ally, an assistant to a boss and a significant team member.

- A secretary is not "just a secretary," but a key staff member with valuable skills.
- A secretary's skills consist of more than typing and shorthand and should be utitilized to their fullest extent.
- A secretary wants and deserves a career-building job.
- Secretaries should be regarded as full-fledged members of the corporate team.
- All secretaries are not alike.

As you take on this progressive perspective, you take your first big step toward finding an assistant who can be a real asset—and, let's face it, you need all the help you can get to succeed in today's competitive business environment.

GETTING READY FOR THE SEARCH

When a manager needs a secretary, it is usually a matter of urgency. The recruitment process is ruled by a sense of "I must get a secretary immediately." It's ironic—while managers are frantic without support, they often give less thought to what to look for in a secretary than they do choosing where to have lunch. You didn't get where you are by jumping into situations without first properly preparing yourself. The same thoughtful deliberation must go into the recruitment process as goes into other important decisions.

Searching for someone to serve as the other half of a work team is, of course, much more involved than looking for a typist. Further, choosing the right support professional is more critical and complex than selecting any other staff member, because your assistant works more closely with you than any other member of your team.

Preparation for the actual search requires developing a composite of the ideal. You need a list of as many adjectives as you can come up with to describe what you need in a secretary—above and beyond mere questions of technical abilities. To imagine your ideal secretary, you need a clear understanding of these factors:

- The nature of your work
- Your work style
- The job you have to offer
- The work setting
- The organizational setting

Your lists will not only help you screen candidates but will also ensure that you, the job, your company and a candidate are all suited to one another. Your outlines will further sell the right candidate, once you've found him or her, on taking the job. You should be as specific as possible in bringing all crucial aspects of each part of the whole out in the open at the outset, leaving nothing to chance.

A secretary who best completes your team is someone who complements your strengths and fills in for your weaknesses. Keep this in mind as you work on your lists. Also think about where you are in the scheme of your career: what your goals are and what you need to achieve them. Choose a support professional who can help you achieve those goals.

ABOUT YOU AND HOW YOU WORK

As you attempt to describe yourself, it's helpful to get the candid opinions of others. It's only human to have a hard time seeing yourself objectively, but distorted perceptions about your personality or work style won't help you hire the right assistant.

Avoid using overly general terms. If you have a reputation as a "difficult" manager, pin down just what "difficult" means. Are you a procrastinator or perfectionist, or have support staff considered you unapproachable? "Difficult" could merely mean you expect a lot of support staff and just have yet to work with one who appreciates you. Now's your chance to set the record straight and hire someone who will thrive on your team because he or she is well suited to it.

Your Work Style

Pinpointing your work style is crucial to hiring a secretary who is compatible with you and will be of most value. Mistakes are commonly made in support staff/manager matching either because managers are unaware of their style or because they assume it's up to the assistant to "adjust." A person's working style is not something that's easily changed. Support staff and managers work too closely together to have incompatible work styles.

And, ideally, your work style and that of your secretary should complement one another where appropriate. You can gain a lot of help and eliminate a lot of anxiety by creating a situation where your secretary picks up your slack. If you're notably disorganized, for example, hire someone who can keep you on track.

To account for any discrepancy between the way you work and the way you think you work, seek out objective input. The following should get you thinking.

When are you most productive? Are you a morning, afternoon or evening person? If you do your best work two hours before everyone else arrives, you'll need a secretary who's also a morning person. If you tend not to get moving until 4:00 in the afternoon, it helps to have a self-starting assistant who can be productive without you leading the way all day. If you're the type who gets most of the work done after everyone else has gone home, you'll either need someone who doesn't mind working frequent overtime or who doesn't mind facing a pile of work on his or her desk first thing in the morning every morning.

Compare your attitude concerning work versus leisure time with that of the prospective assistant. Do you lean more toward the style of a workaholic or a "good-time Charlie"? Consider your expectations of how hard one should work. Do you think people should be busy every minute of an eight-hour day, or do you expect breaks now and then? What is your attitude toward lunch hour? Some people skip lunch without a thought while others feel lunch is an inalienable right. What is your attitude toward overtime? Some feel it is an imposition while others take it as a given. Some expect overtime on short notice while others need to plan for it well in advance.

What is your career versus personal life orientation? Find a secretary whose attitude toward the work/family balance matches yours. Which comes first and how much weight and priority do you give to each? For one person missing a son's baseball game to work overtime is a matter of course, while to another, family comes first no matter what. What is your reaction to time off for family emergencies or just plain family business?

If you are a perfectionist, you will need a secretary who is too. Otherwise, it will drive a secretary crazy when you revise a letter four times or drive you crazy when a letter has to be retyped four times because it's not set up "just so." If you're not a stickler for detail, don't hire an assistant who is—that is, unless you need someone to cover for your bad spelling and grammar. Perfectionists tend to spend more time on projects than nonperfectionists would like, which can create friction.

No one likes to admit to being a procrastinator, but, let's face it, many of us put off the difficult jobs until the eleventh hour. I like to think of this working style in positive terms—some people produce better under pressure. The procrastinator can drive support staff up the wall. But if you do tend toward this style, admit it! What's important is that your assistant understands this about you up front and agrees to put up with it—you can point out your other redeeming qualities to make up for it. Many secretaries put up with the procrastinator in return for other concessions. For example, the secretary who accepts your last-minute emergencies without complaint may appreciate occasional long lunches during slack time for running personal errands. If you are serious about overcoming this habit, find someone who is an excellent time manager and assertive enough to keep on your back about not putting off important projects.

A big question is your delegating style. How much control are you willing to relinquish to your assistant? Do you mind if your assistant edits your work, or do you welcome the help? Are you one to watch over a secretary's shoulder or are you comfortable to leave him or her alone? Do you expect your assistant to remind you of things that need to be done or do you keep track and do the reminding? Are you away from the office a good bit of the time, relying heavily on a secretary to get things done in your absence, or do you prefer to handle things yourself from a distance?

What is your work style under pressure? Do you tend to hide and want to be left alone? Or do you want someone to keep you company through difficult periods. Are you a screamer or the silent type when things get rough? Do you work on one thing at a time and see it through to completion or juggle many projects as you feel inspired? Do you work by the book or are you more the "operator" type who enjoys moving in and around the system?

Personality Blending

When considering personality, bear two points in mind: how a secretary's personality suits your own and how it fits the job.

Finding an assistant whose personality meshes with yours is a tricky business. When it comes to overall personality blending, you may choose to follow either an "opposites attract" or "birds of a feather" philosophy. As you add adjectives to your list, you will notice, as with work styles, that some traits are better matched similarly, others complementarily. For example, two moody people tend to be explosive; if you're the moody type, you'll want a secretary who is particularly even-tempered and able to roll with the punches. In some cases, it's better for you and your secretary to be alike: for instance, if you're a stickler for businesslike formalities, an assistant who yells down the hall for you will drive you crazy. Also look for personality traits you wish you had and seek to fill that lack with your secretary. Here are some traits to get you thinking. Do people consider you:

- Shy or outgoing
- Open or private
- Serious or fun-loving
- Talkative or quiet
- Outspoken or reserved
- Sensitive or aloof
- Businesslike or casual
- Disciplined or carefree
- Rigid or flexible
- Moody or even-tempered
- Energetic or laid back
- Uptight or easygoing

What's most important is that you hire a secretary who complements you in ways that will help you accomplish your work goals and get ahead in your career. For example, manager Susan supervised 10 staff members. Susan was a very private person who found it hard to make the kind of casual "small talk" her subordinates seemed to crave. There was tension between Susan and her staff that made it difficult for Susan to cultivate the team effort she needed to accomplish work goals. The workers in fact took offense at Susan's apparent standoffishness and felt she thought she was somehow "better than them."

Susan wisely hired an assistant with an open friendliness and knack for remembering personal details about people—goings-on at home, outside interests, etc. Susan's secretary, Jane, took on the role of social ambassador on Susan's behalf. As Susan's intermediary, Jane kept up the personalized end of Susan's relationships with her subordinates. Jane would point out to Susan important happenings in staff members' lives and would kick off casual conversations as individuals were coming and going from her office so that Susan could express an appropriate interest—an interest she felt, but just had difficulty expressing on her own.

You also must consider the nature of your work and the personality a secretary needs to succeed in the position. Is your work sales-oriented? Think of sales in a broad sense. Will your secretary be called upon to promote you or your work, service or product to others in person or on the telephone?

Think about whether the secretarial position is a "social" one. Will your secretary need to interact with many others or be more of a loner? Will you and your secretary work as a part of a larger departmental team or more as a solo team within your organization?

Consider the pace of your work. Is it fast-paced, consistent, cyclical or unpredictable? A legal secretary to a labor attorney, for example, must be comfortable working in a chaotic environment, where emergency situations may give rise to heavy workloads on a moment's notice. Another legal secretary working with a real estate attorney may have the leisure of preparing for closings well in advance of closing dates.

THE WORK SCENE

Many factors in the work setting directly affect the work efforts of support staff. The more specific you can be, the better you prepare a prospective secretary for what it would be like to work with you. You should also, of course, point out what are positive aspects of the work setting from a support staff point of view for marketing purposes. Don't try to hide the negatives, however; surprises only lead to problems later.

Let's take a look at your work setting—first, the small picture. Think about how you and your assistant fit into the immediate physical and social surroundings:

- Do you work alone or as part of a larger team?
- How much interaction is there among you and your co-workers? How often will your secretary have to deal with these or other people?

Finding the Best Office Support Professionals • 33

- What kind of people are they? Is it a serious or fun-loving group? Do they tend to be critical and competitive or is it all for one and one for all?
- How do people in the department treat newcomers? Is there an "initiation rite" for new employees before acceptance by the group?
- Do fellow workers pitch in to help each other out?
- Will others help train your assistant or will he or she rely solely on you or have to fend for himself or herself?
- Do higher-ups work nearby or do they tend to stay away?
- Will you share your secretary with one or more other managers? Will any of your subordinates need the secretary's help as well? How many people will the secretary unofficially support?

What about the physical setting in which you work?

- Will your secretary sit out in the open or in some sort of closed cubicle?
- How much room will the secretary have? Are files maintained at the secretary's workstation?
- How close is the secretary's station to your office and the offices of others to whom he or she will report? What kind of intercommunication system will be used?
- Where are support services located in relation to her workstation: i.e., copying center and/or satellite copiers; mail center; receptionist or message center; travel center; any other areas of the building needed to accomplish daily work.
- How many people share the copy machine and other support services?

The physical work setting is of great importance to support staff. Be sensitive to the fact that secretaries don't enjoy sitting clear out in the open, as is often the case. If your assistant will work in some kind of enclosure—or in an office by some rare chance—this is an extremely positive point for you to present. And, of course, the more room a secretary has, the better. If your secretary will not be enclosed or semi-enclosed, maybe there's something you can do to create an illusion of privacy. Perhaps some large plants around the station would help, or you could situate the desk in such a manner as to give the station an air of privacy. Expressing your awareness of the issue is a step in the right direction, in any event.

The availability, proximity and effectiveness of support services is material. A secretary needs to anticipate how much running around during the day will be required to get the job done.

Your Company's "Culture"

Now think about the bigger picture—the organizational setting. You want an assistant who will thrive in the corporate culture of your organization. An organization's culture produces a certain value system as well as norms of behavior to which your secretary must be comfortable adhering.

Attach as many specific descriptive labels to your organization as possible: e.g., laid back, staid, conservative, high risk, fast-paced, constantly changing, high pressure, bureaucratic, growing. For instance, Xerox Corporation sums up its corporate culture by stating this characteristic required of the Xerox employee: "the willingness to be part of the Xerox challenge: ability to handle changing priorities and adjust to a quick turnaround environment."

What values are shared and accepted by employees in your company? Some organizations value conformity, others foster innovation and creativity. In some companies employees feel fortunate just to work for the company. It is a given that the company does a lot for the employees and the employees therefore give the company all they've got—if they want to stay on. Some organizations foster values of security, motivating employees by offering attractive retirement packages. An applicant's background will have a lot to do with how well he or she will fit into your organization.

People are sometimes unaware of the differences between working in various-sized and -configured organizations in terms of culture, rules and unofficial practices which impact on daily work life. Make sure you let a candidate know full well what he or she is in for in order to avoid serious difficulty later. There is undoubtedly a certain way of getting things done in your company. Think of the many unwritten rules you live by in your company and put them on paper. A candidate must know full well what he or she is getting into before coming on board.

Let's look at a disastrous situation in which a highly qualified secretary was hired for a position with no understanding of what the organizational situation would be.

Angela was a top-notch secretary with an associate's degree and five solid years' experience behind her. She had never worked in a corporate environment, and when moving to a new city, decided to give the large company a try. An intelligent woman with excellent technical skills, Angela was quickly hired to fill a middle-level secretarial slot working for five managers: one principal and the four managers who reported to him. She was told it was a "very busy" position, which was great with Angela, who enjoyed a quick-paced environment.

She was totally unprepared, however, for the red tape that would slow her efforts in accomplishing a heavy workload—for instance, rules that governed such simple matters as sending out letters. Accustomed to simply mailing a letter out once it was signed by a manager, Angela now found that letters going out to the "field"—anyone outside of the corporate headquarters in which she worked—required the approval of 11 managers other than those to whom she reported! The official process required filling out and attaching a certain form and forwarding the letter through interoffice mail until it returned with all required approval signatures. After several weeks of frustration over letters taking forever to come back or, worse, getting lost or buried on someone's desk somewhere along the line, Angela finally picked up that common practice is to personally walk a letter through the approval process. Angela was decidedly not the type of person who enjoyed finding ways to work around the "system." Angela stuck it out long enough to earn vacation time and then left for a spot in a much smaller company.

WHAT KIND OF SUPPORT PROFESSIONAL DO YOU NEED?

Think about each of the foregoing considerations (you may find it helpful to refer to the "Checklist/Worksheet" on page 48) and make careful notes of what applies to your situation. Again, the more specific you can be, the better. Next we'll look at what support staff have to offer. Many managers make the mistake of considering a candidate's skills without first pinpointing and prioritizing their own needs. Following is a list of tasks managers might need a secretary or assistant to handle on their behalf.

Check off those needs which apply to you, go back and circle those which are most significant and, finally, prioritize your choices. Add to the list items that are important to you but do not appear below.

MANAGER NEEDS

DOCUMENT PRODUCTION
  Typing, word processing or computer
  Dictation and transcription
  Drafting, editing, proofreading
  Duplication and distribution

TELEPHONE HANDLING
  Screening and routing calls received
  Tracking calls made or received
  Taking messages, gathering and recording necessary information
  Returning calls on manager's behalf

CALENDAR MAINTENANCE AND SCHEDULING
  Scheduling, confirming and reminding manager of appointments
  Coordinating appointments and calendars with other key players
  Recording appointments on more than one calendar

MEETING/CONFERENCE ARRANGEMENTS
  Reserving and setting up meeting rooms
  Preparing agenda and presentation materials
  Taking notes or preparing minutes
  Sending follow-up memos and tracking assignments

INFORMATION/FILE MANAGEMENT
  Storing and retrieving files
  Maintaining database or resource file
  Tracking down needed information
  Reading and summarizing reports
  Analyzing and presenting data

PROJECT ASSISTANCE
  Conducting research
  Fulfilling delegated tasks
  Preparing materials
  Tracking progress
  Managing your time

ADMINISTRATIVE SUPPORT
  Opening, sorting and processing mail
  Making travel arrangements
  Expense reporting
  Financial record-keeping
  Inventory control
  Budget preparation
  Billing

OFFICE MANAGEMENT
  Supervising and training others
  Purchasing office supplies and equipment
  Overseeing maintenance of office equipment

CLIENT OR CUSTOMER RELATIONS
  Greeting and responding to needs of those you serve
  Handling inquiries or complaints
  Involvement in customer service or sales

OTHER
  Making lunch or dinner reservations
  Handling personal matters

EVALUATING SKILLS

Technical Skills—the Basics

Let's talk about support staff skills. You need to be sure a candidate has the technical abilities you require. Make sure, however, that tests used will tell you what you need to know.

Many support professionals are incorrectly judged first and foremost by typing speeds and accuracy. How often have you heard from a personnel counselor, "I've got a great candidate—80 wpm with no errors. Then there's another one who tested 85 wpm but with five errors." It's ridiculous to assign such weight to standard typing tests, first of all, because there is more to a secretary's job than how quickly letters are typed. Further, since most offices today use electronic typewriters, word processors or personal computers, isn't it ludicrous to test typing speed and accuracy on electric typewriters? Not only is the touch different on various keyboards, skewing results, but what's most important is whether a candidate can use the equipment to its maximum effectiveness, not how fast he or she can type on it. The input, formatting and editing of documents on high-tech equipment is a lot more complicated than straight typing on an IBM Selectric. Don't waste your time testing the typing speed of an applicant if what you really need to know is whether he or she can operate a word processor or PC.

Many employers give a spelling test to applicants. I would recommend instead that candidates be tested on their ability to proofread and edit documents. You need a secretary who can pick up errors and correct them: someone who can spot a misspelling and look the word up, not a walking dictionary; someone to correct your grammar so you can focus on content, not form.

What about shorthand skills? The days of one-to-one dictating are on the way out—and are at this point considered a prerogative of only top-level executives. It's a waste of valuable time for both manager and secretary to be drafting a document at the same time. In fact, it's proven more costly. A study by Dartnell Institute of Business Research concluded that it costs $2.78 more per letter when a letter is dictated face-to-face than when it is machine-dictated. While some type of speedwriting skills are valuable for taking down messages and instructions, formalized shorthand is not necessary for this purpose.

The most efficient way to initiate a document is for a manager to enter it directly onto a computer terminal in his or her office. Since this is the practice in only the most progressive companies, that leaves the rest of you to the use of dictating equipment or hand drafting.

In the name of high technology, dictating equipment should be the method of choice, although not all support staff would agree in practice. It's most efficient in principle, assuming you are adept at organizing your thoughts in this manner. Experience shows, however, that not all managers are skillful enough to use dictating equipment without causing serious frustration and distress to the secretary on the receiving end. Some give too few directions, others too many; many leave gaping blanks or erase a few words every time they turn the microphone off to collect their thoughts. Some even write things out first and then dictate the document onto the machine. It makes one wonder whether the studies take into account the frequent less-than-effective use of this equipment.

In any case, you need not ask whether a secretary has

experience with dictating equipment. Anyone can plug it into their ears and type. Besides, no matter how much experience a secretary has with dictating machines, it's rare for anything but the most simple of cover letters to be typed right off the machine into final form. Either the manager makes revisions or the secretary needs to retype letters or other documents because what was typed doesn't look as good as it sounded or because misjudgments were made in formatting. What you should ask, if you use the device, is whether the person will tolerate using it. It's generally not a favorite part of the secretary's job.

If you're not one of the lucky few with your own computer terminal, and your dictating skills are not up to par, it's still acceptable to write things out from many secretaries' point of view, as prehistoric as it may seem. In fact, many secretaries prefer it. There is sometimes a problem with the manager whose handwriting resembles hieroglyphics, yet you'll be surprised how a good secretary will learn to read your scribbles and be proud of the accomplishment. Some actually enjoy the challenge—it's like solving a puzzle.

Other so-called secretarial skills include filing and the use of the telephone. "Filing" is really a term that underemphasizes the enormous task of records and information management, and has become much more complicated since the days when everything was stored manually on paper in filing cabinets. Today's support professional must work within (or even decide upon) a combination of storage methods including various types of microforms (reduced images on film) or within disk computer systems. It's really no longer just "filing"—it's database management and information retrieval systems. You need to know whether a candidate has what it takes to follow whatever system your company uses, or to set up what you need. The best way to find out a candidate's records management abilities is to ask for a description of past experience.

As for the telephone, your concern should go well beyond a pleasant speaking voice. Telephone skills rely heavily on the use of an individual's judgment, tact, knowledge of business etiquette and discretion—and can also rely on more specialized uses. Determine what you need in terms of the telephone—is it sales or customer-service related, or is it courtesy in the face of high-volume calls? Do you rely on your secretary to make calls on your behalf, and if so, what type of calls are they? The best way to evaluate whether a candidate has the telephone skills you need is to set up a typical example and role-play it with the applicant.

A candidate's technical abilities are the easiest secretarial skills to identify. But don't put undue emphasis on a candidate's technical skills—they're only part of the total picture. The other part of that picture is even more crucial to whether a secretary will be of value to you.

Administrative and Discretionary Skills—the Intangible Essentials

Administrative and discretionary skills, largely experience-earned, are less tangible than technical skills, yet comprise the real meat of the seasoned professional's value to the manager. Discretionary skills are those that rely on the use of judgment and the input of each secretary's particular talents:

- Interpersonal skills—the ability to interact and get along well with others;
- Communication skills—the ability to get the message across, both orally and in writing;
- Decision-making skills—the ability to consider alternative courses of action and select the best option for each situation;
- Problem-solving skills—the ability to identify and analyze problem situations, and recommend solutions;
- Information-handling skills—deciding what to do with the massive information that comes across a secretary's desk is key to her success, as well as her boss's; information-handling requires collecting, organizing, prioritizing and channeling it to the appropriate persons;
- Public relations skills—dealing with others, including outside contacts and clients, on the manager's behalf; diplomacy—representing manager and organization to outside world;
- Perceptual skills—serving as the manager's eyes and ears in picking up what's going on around him or her that he or she may be missing but needs to know; also, anticipating the manager's needs without needing to be told;
- Organizational skills—the ability to create order out of

chaos; to keep the manager organized and on track at all times;
- Overall good judgment—the ability to handle situations in the boss's absence or without close supervision in a manner in accord with the boss's wishes; knowing what to say and what not to say; whether to act or to check before taking action; knowing whether and when to interrupt or disturb the boss; knowing when to speak up and when to keep silent.

How discretionary skills apply to a secretary's day-to-day function will be further discussed in Chapter 3. For now, it's important to realize that discretionary skills can be even more important to you than technical skills, even though they are harder to evaluate. You can judge a secretary's level of discretionary skills by how he or she presents her past experience, both on a resume and verbally. But the best information on a candidate's discretionary ability may well come from references. This is why it's important to give more than a perfunctory check into an applicant's previous work history.

Bearing in mind the needs you identified in the last section, review the following list of support staff skills and check off those you seek in the ideal candidate. Once again, review your choices and indicate which skills are most important in order of priority.

SUPPORT STAFF SKILLS

TECHNICAL (BASIC SKILLS)
    English—grammar, spelling
    Other language(s)
    Speed reading
    Dictation and transcription
    Word processing or computers
    Proficiency with other technology (such as fax, electronic mail, other)
    Writing, editing and proofreading
    Presentation
    Accounting and math
    Knowledge of industry and technical terminology
    Business etiquette
    Following instructions
    Understanding organizational structure

ADMINISTRATIVE (SKILLS REQUIRING INDEPENDENT THOUGHT AND ACTION)
Supervising or training
Directing work flow and delegating
Problem-solving and decision-making
Negotiating agreements
Proposing and managing change
Follow-up
Organizing and coordinating
Prioritizing, planning and scheduling
Project management
Setting and meeting goals and deadlines
Managing a heavy workload
Anticipating manager needs
Keeping manager informed
Networking with others
Giving attention to detail

DISCRETIONARY (SKILLS REQUIRING INDIVIDUAL TRAITS, ABILITIES AND TALENTS)
Interpersonal
Listening
Verbal and nonverbal communication
Assertiveness
Public relations
Handling different personality types
Tact and diplomacy
Resolving conflict
Handling pressure
Working as a team with others
Being creative
Learning new things
Maintaining harmonious working relationships
Commitment to quality and professionalism
Balancing big picture perspective with details
Displaying initiative
Logical and disciplined thinking
Good judgment

ALL SECRETARIES ARE NOT ALIKE

As discussed in Chapter 1, a common misconception is that except for differences in mechanical skills, one secretary is about the same as the next. Again, generalized use of the term "secretary" has resulted in a blurring of individuality among those in the profession. Each support professional has his or her own set of abilities, strengths and special talents. Your particular circumstances will determine which candidate is right for you.

Career Versus Noncareer Support Professionals

Let's start by talking about choosing between two basic support staff types: the career versus the noncareer support professional. You may think it's best to avoid noncareer support staff because you expect they will be unhappy and make your life miserable. Or you may think a noncareer secretary will be anxious to leave you for another job.

The reality is that a growing majority of office support professionals do not expect to remain in the profession for the long haul. The single most significant discovery of a 1988 survey of 800 secretaries completed by the Gallup Organization, Inc., was that 61% of respondents saw themselves in a transitional state, striving to management positions or moving toward other fields altogether. Another study conducted by the Katharine Gibbs secretarial school found that 70% of 2,275 students and 4,500 graduates surveyed saw themselves in managerial positions within five years. Twenty percent of the graduates in that study had already moved from secretarial to managerial positions.

It's understandable that you would like to find an assistant who will stay for the long run. But just because a person intends to make the support profession a career doesn't mean he or she will be satisfied with the same job indefinitely. Unless you can continue to offer growth and challenge, the career support professional is just as likely to leave you as the noncareer person.

In any event, it's not always a good idea to be overly focused on finding the long-term secretary. Building a relationship that grows with both of you is one thing. But sometimes a team can stagnate as manager and secretary settle into a status quo. Some managers fall into the trap of finding it more comfortable to go on working with the same person for years on end, even though the relationship may be counterproductive.

Sometimes the secretary who is most willing to stay on year after year is precisely the type you most want to avoid. This is the person who cares above all about collecting a weekly paycheck, is depressed on Monday, can't wait until Friday, and basically cares little about the company, less about your work and not at all about your career. Not only does the unprofessional not care about taking on new responsibilities, he or she resists any deviance from routine, which can cause you more daily frustration than changing assistants every couple of years.

Rather than looking for an assistant who will stay forever, put your energy into finding one who is a good match for you. Above all, remember you want someone who is career-oriented, whether that career is in the support area or not.

Don't be afraid of the stepping-stone secretary. Offering what this person is looking for will provide great incentive for high performance in the name of career advancement. Even if you know from the outset someone will only be with you for a year or two, at least you know that for that year or two you will be getting top-notch assistance.

Think about the job you have to offer. Does it provide opportunity for a support professional to learn about a particular field? If so, it may be just the place for the noncareer secretary.

Within the category of stepping-stone secretary are two basic types: the person shopping for an industry in which to build a career and someone who has chosen an industry and is hoping to get a foot in the door. The shopper wants to learn all there is to know about your field, and is looking for a position which provides large exposure to the meat of the industry. Be honest with yourself and the candidate. If you work in the corporate services division of an advertising agency, your assistant is not likely to learn much about advertising. But if you are an account executive, you have much to offer someone who seeks to learn the ins and outs of the advertising business.

For the person looking to get a foot in the door, again, be honest. The first thing this candidate will ask is whether there is opportunity for advancement in your office. You will, of course, never make promises. A candidate must expect to earn any promotion to be considered in the future. The applicant needs to know whether you have the power to help him or her reach aspirations and whether the position would provide the kind of exposure one would need to ultimately get ahead. If you do have control or can offer exposure, the foot-in-the-door secretary may be a terrific asset to you. He or she will be keenly interested in your work and have great incentive to do a terrific job. As the key to this secretary's ultimate success, you would benefit greatly for the time you work together.

If, however, an applicant seems to expect to get what he or she wants without first earning it, the candidate is being unreasonable and is not the one for you. General time constraints can and should be agreed upon at the outset. It must be a two-way street. You will have much to offer the candidate in return for what he or she is to do for you.

If you're on the fast track and are able to take your assistant along with you, then maybe the career secretary is the one for you. Within the career secretary category, secretaries range from the most green—fresh out of school—to the seasoned professional. Your choice will, of course, be somewhat limited by the salary you can offer. If you're in lower management, chances are you cannot offer salary the seasoned professional will expect—unless you can offer other benefits which make a lower salary palatable (see the section in Chapter 5 on a broad view of compensation).

How Much Experience Do You Really Need?

It seems everyone wants support staff with "experience." But not every manager really needs an assistant with extensive experience. So long as a person has the requisite technical skills, it sometimes pays to hire someone right out of school, with no work experience to speak of.

There are many pluses to working with a green secretary. A brand-new secretary is fresh with enthusiasm and willing to learn. He or she is comfortable on high-tech equipment—that's what students learn on these days—and can probably teach you a few things in that department. New secretaries haven't had a chance to pick up bad habits or to be negatively influenced by the unprofessionals. They are more likely to look to a manager with respect rather than suspicion based on past experience. An inexperienced support person can be molded and brought along more easily than someone seasoned who might have become somewhat set in his or her ways. If an applicant is intelligent and has solid technical skills, that may be all you need to turn a green secretary into someone right for you.

The level of experience you will actually require depends on how much you need to rely on a secretary's administrative and discretionary skills. If you're well organized, for example, and don't need your assistant to keep you on top of what needs to be done, it may pay to consider giving a very green person a chance.

An inexperienced secretary can work very well with a heavy workload in terms of producing documents, correspondence, etc. Here he or she has the chance to display enthusiasm and technical proficiency while learning all about your job, the company and the industry.

But inexperienced support staff may lack the necessary confidence or ability to act without guidance and cannot be expected to jump right in and use independent thought. They are more like sponges, learning on the job and seeking direction from you. A green secretary may not be appropriate if you're too busy to bring him or her up to a working level or if extensive outside contact or in-depth knowledge of your industry is required. But if there are others in the office who can help during the learning period, an inexperienced secretary might work for you.

Managers commonly make the mistake of thinking, "I'm so busy and have so many deadlines, I need a top-notch experienced assistant to help me meet my goals." But a very experienced secretary would be bored to tears in a high-production job, no matter how fast-paced. The experienced career secretary wants to utilize expertise in those hard-earned administrative and discretionary skills, not waste away behind a word processor!

The seasoned professional works best in a situation that allows the exercise of his or her full range of talents—for example, when the manager is frequently out of the office and needs someone to take over in his or her absence. The experienced secretary can keep operations running smoothly while providing you with peace of mind. If you depend on your secretary to keep your head above water when all is coming down around you, the seasoned pro is for you. A secretary with experience has a whole bag of tricks for protecting you from those you don't have time for and to keep you organized in spite of your best efforts to let chaos reign.

Bear in mind, however, that the seasoned professional usually likes to work with little or no supervision. To succeed with the pro, you must be secure enough not to feel threatened (the pro knows his or her place and enjoys it) and be willing to stand back and let your secretary do things his or her own way.

PUTTING IT ALL TOGETHER

You should now have a good understanding of your needs and how a support professional can meet those needs. (Refer once again to your checklists and worksheet on pages 41–42 and 48 to be sure you haven't overlooked anything.) The final step is to prioritize your lists and derive a composite of the ideal secretary to meet your needs.

Listing Your Must Haves and Can't Stands

Read through your lists and label your "must haves." You should use this "must have" list so that you won't waste time on applicants who don't fit the bill and won't make the mistake of hiring someone on impulse who can later turn out to be a nightmare.

Add onto your must-have list those things about you that have perhaps caused problems in the past or that you think might present a problem in the future. Every manager has his or her quirks, and your secretary or assistant must be willing to put up with yours. For instance, if you expect a secretary to perform servile tasks, such as serving coffee, sharpening pencils or running personal errands, it's best to set these things out up front. If you make your expectations known at the beginning, a secretary can look at such tasks as part of the job. But if you treat such sensitive requests as though they were a given, you may come up against serious resistance later as they are viewed as unwelcome chores that interfere with regular duties.

Then think about those characteristics, habits or idiosyncrasies you would put on a "can't stand" list. This is where you articulate what it is about a person that you cannot tolerate—your personal pet peeves. For example:

- Gum chewing/smoking/eating at desk
- Moping/whining/silent treatment
- Being interrupted/scolded/ignored
- Coffee breaks/long lunch hours/clock watching
- Indecisiveness/brashness/insincerity

Your "must haves" and "can't stands" should, of course, be free of characteristics that are covered by equal employment opportunity laws.

Review all of your lists and draw up a profile of the ideal secretary. You should now have a clear idea of what you are looking for, and you're ready to begin the search.

PROFILE OF THE IDEAL SECRETARY
CHECKLIST/WORKSHEET

ABOUT YOU
Work style
- Morning/afternoon/evening person
- Workaholic or good-time Charlie
- Work/personal balance
- How organized
- Perfectionist
- Procrastinator
- Delegating style
- Style under pressure
- Project juggler
- "Operator" or "by the book"

Personality
Strengths/weaknesses
Quirks

ABOUT THE JOB
Industry
Size of department
Physical setting
Social environment
Number of managers to be assigned to secretary
Support services
Work pace
- Fast/slow
- Consistent
- Cyclical
- Unpredictable

Sales, service or product oriented
Goals
Overtime

ABOUT THE COMPANY
Size
Location
Configuration
Corporate culture
- Progressive
- Conservative
- Creative
- Laid back
- Staid
- High pressure
- Growing
- High risk

Values
Policies/practices
Rules and regulations
Unwritten rules
Benefits

THE SECRETARY YOU SEEK

Career or stepping-stone (shopper or foot-in-the-door)
Background
Level of experience
Personality
Technical skills
Discretionary skills
Special talents

MUST HAVE	CAN'T STANDS
_____	_____
_____	_____
_____	_____
_____	_____
_____	_____
_____	_____
_____	_____
_____	_____

PROFILE OF THE IDEAL
_____
_____
_____
_____
_____
_____
_____

WHERE AND HOW TO LOOK FOR YOUR SECRETARY
Shopping Within Your Company

A good source of support staff may be your own company. If a secretary is unhappy in a given position, it's better to keep that secretary within the company than have to fill two places from the outside instead of one. Cost estimates for replacing secretaries run from $7,500 to $10,000 when you include the selection process, training and the learning curve. Hiring a secretary who already works for the company not only saves you the valuable time and effort involved in recruiting from the outside, but also spares you the trouble of finding someone who fits your organization and reduces the learning curve considerably.

Some companies encourage support staff to move around within a company through job posting systems. If you work for such a company, you may be lucky to find the mechanism already in place to help you. To make the most of a job posting system, get as involved as possible in the posting process. Write your own position description rather than leaving that task to the Personnel Department and be as specific as you can. Don't be limited in what you say by a form that's given to you for this use.

Make sure word gets out about your opening through the grapevine as well as through the official process. The perfect candidate may not actively be looking for a new position and miss seeing your posting, but still be interested in the right opportunity. Review applicant responses yourself—don't just rely on what you are told by Personnel—and make your own inquiries about people who are interested in the job.

Even if your company does not have a posting system or otherwise openly encourage transferring from within, you can still "shop" for an assistant within your organization. Notice the secretaries with whom you come in contact. Don't necessarily look for someone who is so obviously unhappy he or she is shouting it from the rooftops—dissatisfaction can be hidden under a smile. A secretary doesn't necessarily have to be unhappy to be interested in a new opportunity. Even someone who has been with a certain boss or department for a long time may be fair game. Anyone who is serious about career advancement will be open to hearing about an interesting opportunity, which, of course, you have to offer.

If you see someone you think might be right for you, it

doesn't take much to find out whether that person would be interested in hearing about the position you have to offer. Discreet inquiries can be made, through your network of trusted friends or other support staff with whom you are familiar. If you work in a company where support staff don't change managers as a matter of course, you'll have to think about the possible repercussions of your actions. Stealing an assistant from another manager can sometimes create awkward situations. You would, of course, have to weigh the political consequences of your actions. Ruffled feathers can be smoothed over most easily when the transfer could be considered a promotion for the secretary. If it's a lateral move, changing departments for variety serves as another allowable circumstance. Your only potential trouble is if the secretary's current manager has real and dangerous power over your career. Some people take it very personally when they lose a secretary to another manager within the company, and an abandoned boss could become vengeful. You would, of course, have to consider that possibility.

If you don't know of anyone you would like to win away, it's still a good idea to tap into the organizational grapevine and get word out about the fantastic position you have to offer. Someone may surface you didn't think of. Remember, though, it's on the grapevine that you need to sell yourself and the position so that word of your opening will be passed on in a good light (see "Marketing the Job," page 64). Here's where it becomes important for you to have the reputation of a "good boss." It's commonly known that the only way for a secretary to get into some companies from the outside is to take a job that absolutely no one on the inside wants. You wouldn't want that designation tied to your secretary's position.

If a search within the company fails, it's time to begin your outside search.

Dealing with the Personnel Department

If you are required to go through Personnel to hire an assistant, you must still take an active role in the search and selection process. The Personnel Department is there to serve you; your personnel representative can serve you best when he or she clearly understands your needs. Nothing is more frustrating for a personnel representative than to send up candidate after candidate only to have them all rejected by a manager who can't give specific reasons for his or her disapproval. Your representative should certainly appreciate your help—after all, it's you he or she is trying to please.

To start with, become friendly with your personnel representative so that he or she knows you personally and not as just as a name on a requisition form. Be sure you clearly understand the recruiting method to be used. Will the position first be offered to employees within the company? If so, you will want to be involved, as previously discussed. Will an agency be used for outside recruiting? If so, you might want to recommend an agency you have learned has a good reputation. In fact, you might also let your personnel rep know about all the sources you've discovered. Ask if the position will be advertised. If so, send a draft of the ad you would like to appear (see page 52, "Advertising Successfully").

The usual procedure is for the Personnel Department to do the initial screening of candidates and then for you to select from a group of semifinalists. Choosing your assistant is far too important to leave in the hands of a third party—don't sit and wait for what someone else considers to be the two or three best candidates for your position. Get involved right from the start.

Make what you seek in an assistant as clear as possible. Use the profile you created in the previous section to give your personnel rep a specific description of your ideal candidate. Once you're sure you're understood, let Personnel do what they do best—testing for basic skill levels and screening for other organizational requirements. But don't be unduly influenced by test scores unless you understand the testing used. Ask to see the tests administered and decide for yourself whether they are meaningful in your case.

With your guidance, a personnel representative can accomplish the tedious narrowing of the applicant field. Let the personnel rep handle the paperwork; you do the interviewing. Only you can decide which candidate is right for you.

If your secretary will report to other managers besides you, you should still get involved in the selection process; in fact, the more influence you exert, the better. Everyone dreads looking for a secretary. And a principal who has the responsibility for hiring someone to please others in addition to himself has an added burden. Share the insight you have gained in moving through this analysis process with the other managers, especially with whoever has decision-making authority.

If you do not have the authority to choose the secretary, don't throw up your hands and leave the selection to fate! Put yourself in the active role. More than likely, the principal has not thought out the selection process as carefully as you have. The principal will probably welcome your help in outlining a selection process—you will probably be raising items he or she never thought of or didn't take the time to work through.

If you cannot control the selection process, look at your must-have/can't-stand lists and circle those characteristics that are most important to you. Then share your list with the principal and, if appropriate, the other managers to whom the secretary will report. If you work in the same area, in effect on the same team, you may gain support that will be even more helpful in influencing Personnel with decisions made at their end.

Advertising Successfully

It is usually the case that many more advertisements for secretarial openings appear on a given day than one person can or will respond to. It's therefore up to you to write an ad that will catch a reader's eye in spite of all the other ads on the page. Your emphasis in the ad should be twofold: (1) marketing the job and your company and (2) making the candidate feel special before he or she even applies for the job.

Since many secretaries suffer from poor organizational treatment, it helps if your company can boast a better-than-average environment for support staff. For example, start the ad with something like, "Join a company that's terrific to its support staff. . . ." You could then go on to describe specifically what makes your company good to work for: "We offer comprehensive benefits including dental, profit sharing, bonus . . ." etc. It's a good idea to list any benefit you will offer, especially those that reflect a progressive outlook on the profession: "Opportunity is encouraged for personal and professional growth—tuition reimbursement and on-the-job training. . . ."

Choice of Title. "Executive assistant," "executive secretary," "administrative assistant," "administrative secretary," or just plain "secretary" are titles commonly used in advertisements. Probably the most desirable title from a professional secretary's point of view is "executive assistant." However, this title really implies a position of the highest level. "Executive secretary" is more a generic term, although it does still have some connotation of requiring greater-than-average experience. "Administrative assistant" is a term that was introduced in response to the fact that so many talented people looking for jobs don't want to be considered "just a secretary." All the term does is focus on the administrative aspects of a secretary's job rather than the strictly secretarial. But since most support staff carry out administrative functions to some degree, the term is really nothing more than a euphemism. Most applicants recognize that this title does not necessarily signify a more prestigious position. What's most important is how you describe the position, not what you call it. Look at the publication you intend to use and see what heading is most commonly used. If more than one heading contains a substantial number of ads, read them closely to determine which category would better describe your position.

Discussion of Salary. Applicants do sift through ads based on salaries offered; you must, therefore, say something about salary or you will get no response. However, unless you are offering top dollar, don't mention a specific salary range. If you state a salary in the median range, you will be lumping your position in with all the others in that same range rather than setting yourself apart. Be vague but seductive: "Salary commensurate with experience" is often used, and considered by some to be encouraging. I recommend using "competitive salary." It's much more inviting.

Your Industry. It's a good idea to mention your industry to spark the interest of a candidate. Don't, however, make the mistake of requiring overly specific experience in a specialty of your field. What you need is a person who will fit into the basic environment, and broad experience in your general field will satisfy that requirement. For example, a secretary who is familiar with banking can certainly learn what it takes to handle a job in loan documentation. Or a legal secretary with experience in real estate can quickly learn new terminology and procedures necessary for bankruptcy—what's critical is that the secretary be familiar with the legal environment. A secretary's skills are easily transferable—what's important is that the candidate have an interest in what you do and be motivated to learn. Don't overlook the fact that many secretaries are seeking a job change simply because they are bored with what their experience has encompassed. Once a secretary has mastered a certain field and has advanced as far as possible within that field, the challenge and stimulation of learning a new specialty may be just what is needed.

Describing the Job. First and foremost, don't discuss "secretarial skills" required. It's a real turnoff to read "55 wpm required"—one gets the impression all there is to do is type. You can screen for skill levels later—first get the candidate's attention. Choose one catchy phrase to set the mood: "challenging and rewarding role"; "project-oriented position"; "unusual opportunity." Then focus on the interesting aspects of the job, being somewhat specific: "coordinating flow of activities"; "planning and promotion of special events"; "managing day-to-day departmental operation." Overly general phrases such as "diverse position" tell the reader nothing. If the position you offer is entry-level, say "growth position."

Don't fail to mention any special features that set the job apart from the pack: advantageous location; near transportation or shopping; plush offices; discounts or perks offered to employees, etc.

About the Ideal Candidate. Whatever you say should in effect be a compliment in advance to the applicant. This shows you appreciate the difference between an average secretary and the true professional: i.e., "Seeking polished professional," or "Top-flight assistant needed." "Career-minded" or "career-oriented individual" has been done to death.

Reference to a "commendable work history" is far superior to asking for specific experience. Restrictions of an arbitrary three or five years' experience in a certain area may well keep a less experienced yet highly motivated candidate from inquiring, so it's best not to get too specific.

Some other terms that are overdone: "bright" (or "brite"), "energetic," "self-starter," "detail-oriented" (I'm not even sure what this means, but it sounds boring). Instead use: "ambitious," "motivated," "take-charge," "work-on-own type," "independent," "creative," "intelligent." Use phrasing that shows some thought went into the ad, giving a more personalized touch: "We need someone with a special combination of intelligence, enthusiasm and sense of humor to complete our fast-paced team."

Inviting Inquiry. If you are in an area where competition for candidates is extremely stiff, giving a phone number to call provides most immediacy. Candidates are more likely to pick up the phone to inquire than to write to an address or box number. If you've written a longer, detailed ad that really sells the position, consider using an address or box number. One school of thought is that really serious candidates will take the time to write. In any event, it's best from your point of view to screen initial inquiries by resume. Resumes are particularly helpful as applied to secretaries since you can tell a lot just by how the resume is organized, how professional it looks in general and whether the spelling and grammar of the candidate are up to par. If you decide to go the phone route, you can still invite those who pass initial screening to send in a resume in order to be considered. If they're serious, they'll follow through.

Getting Help: Selecting an Agency

You may decide you need help with the recruitment process. You must be very careful about your choice of agency or your recruiting experience can be nothing but a frustrating waste of time. Here are some pointers for selecting an agency that will truly be a help rather than a hindrance.

Until recently, most agencies dealing in support staff were of the placement variety. Such firms operate by collecting applicants and placing as many of them as possible. As job orders come in, the agency searches its files to find an applicant who might be right for the position. When an applicant walks in or responds to an advertisement, the agency goes through its job orders and tries to find a position suitable for that person.

New on the secretary recruiting scene is the executive secretary search firm. The services of this type of agency are more streamlined toward client needs. Executive secretary search operates in the tradition of executive recruiting: real "searches" are conducted through accessing a network of contacts and following up on leads to find the right secretarial candidate for a client.

Recruiting agencies for secretaries are scarce at this time. It's a segment of the industry that is just developing in response to the increasing demand for top-flight secretaries during times of critical shortage of candidates to meet that need. It's well worth your effort to seek out the true recruiting agency, however, since the typical placement agency experience is often a nightmare.

Ideally, agencies act as middleman between employers and applicants, purportedly as matchmaker, effecting a "fit" between manager and applicant. You call an agency and place a job order, explaining in detail what you are looking for. On the other end, you might assume, the agency will serve as a sort of career counselor to applicants, providing guidance in choosing the right job. The truth is, secretarial placement, especially in metropolitan areas, is really a cutthroat business—many agencies care not about creating a match, just earning a commission.

One thing to remember: It's just as hard for agencies to find top-notch candidates as it is for you. And since placing support staff is its business, an agency must try to place whatever candidates it has in order to pay the rent. Many use the "shotgun" approach: a rep will send you a trail of applicants a mile long, but none of them will remotely resemble what you thought you ordered. After a while, you start to think the person you seek isn't out there, and you lower your standards. Finally, out of sheer exasperation, you hire the best of the lot even if you really don't feel the applicant is right for the job.

Here's how it goes from the applicant's point of view. Candidates are lured in by seductive advertisements about fantastic jobs with great salaries and benefits. The chance that the applicant will get to interview for that job is slim to none—if the job even in fact did exist, by the time the applicant enters the office, it may well have been filled. Once the candidate is in the office, the agency will listen to what a candidate thinks he or she wants, and then, as if they didn't hear a word that was said, give the applicant a rundown on what jobs they have to offer. The agency will use every trick in the book—cajole, persuade, make the applicant feel guilty—to get him or her to go on as many interviews as possible. Then, pressure is high for the candidate to accept the first job that's offered.

If secretaries were abundant, agencies would be competing with one another for corporate clients and be more likely to provide the kind of personal attention you need. In light of the shortage, however, agencies compete more for applicants than job orders. Many an agency's goal is to get an applicant hired and keep that person hired until they collect their commission—about three months. After that, it's not unusual for agencies to start calling the candidate to go on another set of interviews with promises of even higher pay and better benefits.

Plus, here's an industry where computerization has in some ways served to worsen service to clients rather than improve it. By computerizing job orders, the so-called "counselors" within the agency can access all open positions known to the firm. Right off the bat, the agency representative who accesses the job order may be telling applicants about a client or industry they really know nothing about. Often the job data is sketchy—the software program allows only a certain amount of information to be entered in about each job order—or, worse, the information is completely inaccurate. A frequent complaint is that applicants take time off from work to go out on an interview only to find that the job has been filled or is not at all what he or she is looking for.

Of course, not all agencies fit the above description. It does seem, however, that this type is the most visible, and most accessible to both clients and applicants, since it relies heavily on advertising. You must take the time to find an agency that truly cares about serving you, the client. Your first clue about an agency is whether you are given any personal attention when you call to place an order. Notice whether you are asked for particulars about your company and the job you are offering or whether you get the feeling the rep is trying to finish up with you as fast as possible. The rep should be willing to take the time for in-depth discussion about you, the position, your company and the person you seek. A counselor who is interested in hearing numerous details will presumably pass that information along to applicants.

Check into the credentials of the counselor. Personnel consultants or agencies who belong to the National Association of Personnel Consultants are likely to be reliable and ethical. It's a good idea to seek personnel consultants who hold the CPC (Certified Personnel Consultant) certificate. To obtain this certification, one must have two years' experience in a private placement firm, subscribe to the National Association of Personnel Consultants' Code of Ethics and pass an extensive examination on employment agency law and personnel consulting practices.

There are those in the industry whose efforts not only serve you, the client, but also work toward enhancing the secretarial profession and the recruitment process. Consultants and agencies who are Associate Members of Professional Secretaries International may be particularly qualified in this regard. Seek those recruiters who not only have extensive recruiting experience but also bring to the job past direct experience as executive secretaries, allowing greater understanding of what it takes to create a successful manager/secretary match. The representative should also know something about your industry in general and the equipment to be used in your office in particular. This will help ensure your agency experience will be a positive one.

All agencies conduct skill testing, but be sure you understand the scope of such tests and ask to see actual results—don't rely on what you are told over the phone. Also, find out what their specialty is, if they have one. Some agencies deal primarily in certain industries; other handle specific position levels, either on the low or high end.

If you have doubts about the agency, a good check is to ask the applicants sent to you what their experience has been. More applicants than you can believe withstand horrendous treatment by agencies—basically because they don't understand how the recruitment process should work, and because they are uninformed about their own choices in searching for a job. You can learn a lot just by asking the people you interview—if he or she volunteers a choice horror story, your doubts about an agency may be confirmed.

Your best bet is to locate a professional secretary search firm. Recruiting firms that conduct a professional executive secretary search in the tradition of executive recruiting are few and far between, but worth the effort of finding. Again, the key term here is "search" rather than "placement." Professional executive secretary search firms rely on referral networks for candidates rather than drawing from advertising. And it's often the case that not every applicant is placed who walks through the door. Applicants must meet stringent requirements before even being considered by some firms as a candidate.

The most elite of secretarial recruiting firms deal only in placing "executive assistants" with upper-level executives. With this type of serious search firm, involvement in the recruiting process goes well beyond the typical initial screening and skill testing of applicants. In working to find a real "match" between executive and secretary, these firms focus not only on basic job requirements, but also on the psychological aspects of the executive and what kind of secretary best meets his or her needs. Going beyond usual reference checking, this type of firm, such as the Duncan Group in New York City, thoroughly investigates a candidate's reputation in the business world through a network of contacts. With top-level firms, the recruitment process is so comprehensive that the client executive is finally presented with two or three candidates all of whom are considered not semifinalists, but equally perfect for the job. The client then only has to choose which one he or she likes best, rather than spend any time evaluating the candidates.

Of course, such personalized service is expensive. The ultimate in executive secretary recruiting firms work on a retainer, rather than contingency, basis. To give you an idea of fee ranges, the average agency charges 10% to 15% of the candidate's annual salary, payable when the candidate has remained on the job three months. Executive search firms charge up to 30% of annual salary, with those operating on a retainer basis requiring half that amount in advance and the remainder becoming due if and when an applicant is hired.

If a retainer is more than you are willing to spend or if the secretary you seek is not at the highest executive level, you can still get proper treatment from a firm that operates on search principles, but still on a contingency basis. A tip for initial screening: Find out whether the agency sees applicants strictly on an appointment basis. If not, chances are the agency is not operating at the sophisticated level you seek.

Secretarial Schools

Another good source of applicants is support staff training grounds. Many corporate recruiters have already caught on to gaining a competitive edge by approaching schools that train secretaries well in advance of graduation day. Secretaries are trained in many two-year state colleges and many private business, technical and secretarial schools. Most, if not all, schools have a placement office where employers can place job orders and learn about potential candidates. Some placement offices charge a fee, although most do not.

Tapping the Secretarial Networks

See the Appendix for a list of support staff associations, which often prove a valuable source of potential candidates.

MAKING THE "RIGHT" CHOICE

You're well armed with a profile of what you need in a support professional and with leads for where to find the perfect person to complete your work team. Now you need some tips on weeding through candidates, recognizing the right one for you and convincing that person to accept the job you have to offer.

Prescreening a Candidate

We've talked at length about specifics. Now let's step back and look at how you'll know whether an applicant is in the running from your first contact.

There are, of course, the usual attributes one looks for in a job candidate: positive attitude, reliability, initiative, honesty, diligence, etc. When choosing a secretary, however, your first and foremost concern is whether the secretary exhibits professionalism.

How do you identify an unprofessional? First, by appearance. The true professional knows enough to wear a business suit to an interview; the exceptional candidate will have researched appropriate attire for your particular office and dressed accordingly. Everyone can be expected to know that one should look one's best when interviewing for a job. Therefore, don't give someone the benefit of the doubt when it comes to appearance. If that's the best they can do, imagine what they'll look like on a regular basis.

Next, pay attention to what the applicant says and how he or she says it. How does the applicant describe previous jobs? Does the candidate seem proud of what he or she has accomplished or only think of past performance in terms of previous bosses' jobs? Does the applicant seem enthusiastic about the opportunities your job might offer or just interested in how much money it pays? Does the candidate have ideas for future career plans, or is it evident their attitude is "I think about one job at a time"?

Tone of voice conveys more than words themselves. Does the applicant's tone of voice convey confidence? Does the candidate sound calm and in control or nervous beyond what one might expect from an interviewee in general? You want someone who values their own ability to make a contribution. Look for someone who sounds able to do just that.

So much for evaluating surface clues. Your next consideration has to do with how a secretary can help you get ahead in your career. You need a secretary who understands the concerns of managers and management in general—someone who understands the importance of relating to company goals, not only self-interests.

The way to determine an applicant's perspective is to ask the simple question: "Tell me about the companies you have previously worked for." If the candidate can intelligently discuss the company's business, goals and status in the marketplace, you're okay. If the applicant goes on at length about benefits, compensation or vacations, you're in trouble.

Another important consideration is whether a secretary's locus of control lies within rather than outside his or herself. You can't benefit from secretaries who see past experience as a series of events that happened to them rather than situations they had a hand in controlling. Candidates who have long lists of reasons why past jobs were so unsatisfying and none of the reasons involve their own contribution are likely those who see themselves victims of circumstances rather than creators of reality.

There is one exception to keep in mind. Don't pass up what you think might be an "unpolished gem." Try to tell the difference between someone whose established set of characteristics is undesirable and one who can be molded into the ideal. The unpolished gem might come across as eager to learn, although somewhat naive.

One final crucial point to keep in mind. Be extremely concerned about an applicant's discretion. Never consider hiring a secretary who bad-mouths previous bosses. Take it as a clue that you'll never know what that person will say about you. Don't eliminate a candidate just because of a previous personality conflict between secretary and manager, but how an applicant chooses to relate the situation will reveal just how discreet you can expect that person to be.

Reading a Resume—Between the Lines

When it comes to screening office support professionals, you can learn much more about a candidate from a resume than past job experience—it is, in fact, a useful guide of a secretary's level of professionalism and perspective. Pay close attention to how a resume looks as well as its content. If a secretary's resume isn't highly eye-appealing, it's a serious comment on what kind of support person he or she is. It should be virtually perfect—set up attractively, no typos, no white-out (yes, I've seen it!) and carefully organized. It should reflect a true understanding of what duties were performed in previous jobs. If a resume lists only the usual secretarial duties—typing, filing, etc.—it's a clue that that candidate is unaware of how a secretary can function as a real team member and oblivious to the importance of discretionary duties. If, on the other hand, a resume reflects insight into how a secretary contributed on the job, it's a good sign he or she will be able to do the same for you.

Notice whether descriptive paragraphs mention the business or industry of the employer. See if there is mention of the department in which the candidate worked. If the resume is nothing more than a chronological listing of past jobs, but it at least looks perfect, you may give the candidate an opportunity to provide in-depth explanation of experience.

Prescreening by Telephone

The telephone has limited use in the interviewing process. It's an extremely imperfect device for communication and is not an effective way to evaluate candidates. A person's voice tends to bring to mind a picture that rarely resembles the person on the other end, either from a positive or negative point of view. Ideally, the telephone should be used only for the purpose of inviting candidates to forward a resume and cover letter.

If you are inundated by phone calls in response to an advertisement (lucky you!), you may want to use the telephone to determine whether an applicant will get to first base. To weed out unlikelies from the start, be systematic, rather than subjective, about it. Choose items from your "must have" or "can't stand" list to use as a guide. For instance, one management consulting firm in New York City started out by asking every female applicant who called whether they had a problem with wearing stockings every day—even in the height of summer in the city. This is not the time to get into lengthy discussions of background or details about your position. You want to avoid prejudging an applicant in terms of past experience or skill levels—you could pass up someone special if you decide an applicant's experience is too light without even meeting him or her. If a caller's first questions has to do with money, you can feel confident ruling that candidate out, however. You want someone who is interested in a career-building job, not just bringing home a paycheck.

If you insist on prescreening by phone, a good method is to ask each caller a good open-ended question like "What is your situation" to get them talking. You won't learn anything if they ask the questions and you do the talking. Decide in advance on objective criteria you seek to learn as a result of the phone call. Again, when using the phone, don't rely on subjective reactions or you could be wasting your time or, worse, making false judgments.

The One-on-One Interview

You know what you want to find out. Let's talk about how you'll find out whether an applicant fits the bill. First of all, be prepared: have your lists at hand and an agenda in mind. And don't wait until the applicant is sitting in front of you to review the resume. Read it in advance, and take notes—if you're reading many resumes and interviewing a lot of people, you won't remember what it was you meant to ask.

Avoid falling into the trap of applicants who say things they think you want to hear. You want an assistant who is as concerned as you that the support staff/manager match be right.

I recommend, again, the use of open-ended questions that provide you with the opportunity to evaluate candidates based on their method and comfort in handling the response. You can uncover their level of self-confidence, how articulate they are, whether they have a positive or negative attitude, whether they talk too much or too little, how discreet they are—all in addition to learning whatever's on your lists. Some ideas:

- "Tell me about your last job."
- "Tell me what you learned on your last job."
- "Tell me about your favorite boss."
- "Tell me what you're looking for in a job."

Don't ask what interests the applicant in your position—at least not until after he or she has had a chance to learn something about it. One purpose of the interview should be for the candidate to learn what the job has to offer. The candidate should show an interest in learning what the job entails, rather than just attempt to convince you to hire him or her for the job.

One good way to find out whether a person's working style is compatible with your own is to set up a hypothetical working situation and let the candidate tell you how he or she would handle it. The president of an advertising agency used this approach. He described a scenario in which the secretary would be required to make a decision in his absence that included whether or not to contact him. By her answer, he was able to determine whether they were on the same wavelength.

Another good technique is to arrange in advance for someone to enter your office while you are interviewing the candidate. Introduce the guest to the applicant. How the candidate reacts will tell you a lot about his or her level of confidence, ability to relate to others, sense of business etiquette, and in general, whether you are comfortable with that candidate's style.

Don't feel you must decide on a candidate after just one in-person interview. It's good enough for a first step to get a general sense about whether or not someone is in the running. You can then make notes and start the narrowing process on the next round. Invite the applicant to come back again in a few days, assuming, of course, that time allows and that the person is not pressured to act on another offer. In the next day or so, you may well think of things you wish you had said or asked.

Picking a Winner

By the time you get down to choosing between two or three candidates, you should have covered absolutely everything on your list. Don't get hung up on one issue to the neglect of others, and leave no stone unturned.

When it comes down to choosing between two or three semifinalists, chances are there will be pros and cons to each. That's when it's time to sleep on it and use your intuition. If logic tells you to pick one over another, but something nags at you to choose another candidate, follow that feeling. It is undoubtedly based on information you're carrying but are not openly aware of—the reason will reveal itself in time. If you ignore your inner voice, you may likely find yourself sorry later.

Marketing the Job

Now that you've zeroed in on the best candidate, you must convince that person to accept your offer.

Speak to the candidate as a colleague, show you consider support staff to be a part of your "team." Tell the candidate about the job in as much detail as possible. The more a person knows about a situation in advance, the less anxiety he or she will feel about entering into it. If the secretary you want is deciding between your job and another one, chances are that candidate will go with what is the surer bet.

Convey overall that you are a progressive-minded boss who will treat the secretary as a significant part of the team. When describing the job, emphasize the administrative aspects of the position. Don't discuss the filing system or word processing equipment. Tell the candidate what is accomplished by your company, your department, and about the types of projects you get involved in. Give examples of particularly rewarding situations you experience. Talk about the other people with whom the secretary will come in contact—emphasizing their good points. If your company will provide in-house training or pay for continuing education or seminars of any kind, let the candidate know that fact.

Of course, you shouldn't promise a rose garden. Give the candidate as realistic an idea as possible what it would be like to work with you. Be completely up front, including the negatives as well as the positives—trying to hide the downside of the job will only create suspicion. Once you've made clear the overall scope, reveal special requirements of the job that might meet with resistance if left to chance: e.g., if you expect your secretary to do all of your copying, place all of your telephone calls, or, yes, let's not forget to mention, serve coffee. Your overall message should be positive, yet realistic.

Encourage the secretary to give you and the company a try.

Making the Offer

Avoid the nightmare of finding the perfect candidate only to lose out to another offer. When you make the offer, do it yourself, don't have Personnel make the call. The personal touch means a lot. If you can make the offer in person, do so. That way, you will have the opportunity to pick up on the applicant's reaction to your offer and be able to clear the air about anything that is not agreeable to the candidate right on the spot. Small things that may not matter to you can lose you a candidate who is choosing between two jobs. Don't let anything slip through the cracks. Make it clear that negotiation in no way obligates the candidate to accept—you're just making sure you've done all you can to win the candidate over. If you've covered all bases and the candidate still chooses another job, at least you know there were no unanswered questions. You can then continue your search without nagging doubts.

# BUILDING AN EFFECTIVE SUPPORT STAFF/ MANAGER TEAM

WHAT DO SECRETARIES REALLY DO?

Myth versus Reality

If someone were to ask you what a secretary does, what would you answer? More than likely, your response would reflect the perception gap between what secretaries are believed to do and how they actually contribute on the job.

Most people, including many support professionals themselves, are hard pressed to describe what they do beyond the obvious—type, take dictation, file, answer the telephone. The myth also includes stereotypical "office wife" duties: water the plants, serve coffee, order the boss's lunch and shop for the spouse's birthday present. Ironically, although the term "secretary" is used so broadly as to encompass almost any office worker who uses the typewriter, one still tends to have this single stereotypical image in mind when hearing the word. The truth is that there are as many different support professionals as there are support positions, and just as vast an array of duties and responsibilities that go along with them.

Do support staff type, file, serve coffee and run errands? Yes, secretaries do some form of "typing" either on word processing equipment, a computer or typewriter. And, yes, many secretaries do serve coffee and perform other service-oriented tasks—and there's nothing wrong with that if it makes sense in a particular job. But this doesn't mean that's all support staff do. To make the most of your secretary or assistant, you must move beyond the stereotypical view of a secretary's function and recognize all that a support professional can do for you in a real value-added role. Let's take apart the job of secretary and see what really goes on.

A survey conducted by *Working Woman* magazine in September 1985 addressed the issue of what secretaries actually do. The survey listed 21 duties ranging from the most menial (serving coffee, sharpening pencils, ordering lunch) to what was termed "high-level tasks" (draft letters, troubleshoot, do research, edit/write reports, prepare the budget, supervise others). The survey results reflected a significant gap between what responding secretaries said they are expected to do and what responding bosses say secretaries are expected to do (see table below).

**Two Different Worlds:
Do Bosses Really See What Secretaries Are Doing?**

Secretaries and bosses report radically different versions of what a secretary is "expected" to do.

HIGH-LEVEL TASKS	**Secretaries**	**Bosses**
Draft letters	86%	57%
Troubleshoot	73	47
Do research	65	37
Edit/write reports	58	26
Supervise/train receptionist, etc.	41	33
Prepare the budget	23	10
THE "SERVILE SIX"		
Clean coffeepot	45	31
Sharpen pencils	45	32
Make personal arrangements for boss	39	17
Run personal errands for boss	38	17
Get boss's lunch	29	17
Balance boss's checkbook; pay his/her bills	13	5

Reprinted with permission from *Working Woman* magazine. Copyright © 1986 by Working Woman, Inc.

Note that while there is a significant gap between what secretaries say they are expected to do and what managers say secretaries are expected to do, this gap is most notable when it comes to the performance of higher-level tasks. As *Working Woman* concluded: "The time for American managers to give their secretaries credit for the true nature of their work seems long overdue." A membership study conducted in 1988 by Professional Secretaries International found similar results. Of 1,200 respondents, 36% reported that they supervise others and 52% reported that they train others.

As these surveys suggest, there is much more to the support staff role than typing and filing, or even drafting letters and preparing the budget.

Technical, Administrative and Discretionary Skills in Action

In Chapter 2, we discussed three basic types of secretarial skills. Now let's take a closer look at how these skills contribute on a day-to-day basis.

To recap, we're using the term "technical skills" to indicate those skills usually connected with support staff, such as typing, filing and answering the telepone. Grammar, spelling and familiarity with technical or industry-specific terminology are also technical skills that benefit the manager, yet often go unrecognized.

Administrative and discretionary skills are largely experience-earned, rely on the use of judgment and are hard to measure yet invaluable to a boss. Discretionary skills also encompass the particular talents a secretary brings to the job. Each support professional exhibits a unique blend of both types of skills in his or her daily work. Administrative, discretionary and technical skills are not separate and distinct from one another, but rather work together for the benefit of the manager. Here are some examples.

Typing. Mastering sophisticated word processing or computer equipment and software applications—the norm rather than the exception nowadays—is no simple task. It's one thing to simply type into sophisticated word processing or computer equipment and quite another to take full advantage of what a system has to offer. Word processors or word processing software packages provide a myriad of functions that can be utilized only if the operator has the patience and interest to learn such capabilities, and, even then, only if the individual is capable of thinking like a computer, so to speak. It's not a talent every person possesses!

Whoever has the impression it doesn't take brains to be a secretary is way off base—even when talking about this basic technical area.

And what of the pages that are typed? There's more to preparing an attractive presentation or proposal than just typing words on a page. "Creative typing," as I call it, takes an artistic sense of sorts, and a pride in making the extra effort to create a document that is a step above the rest. It's certainly not news that no matter the quality of a document's contents, the way it is presented has a significant impact on how it will be received by the reader.

Filing. Filing is an outdated term that once described the function of putting pieces of paper in appropriately labeled folders for later retrieval. In the "information age," filing has taken on a different meaning and added new value to the secretary's role. What was once called "filing" has now evolved into "records management," "information retrieval," or, in some cases, "database management." Even the most straightforward of records management systems require keen organizational and decision-making skills so that a manager can have instant access to whatever information he or she needs at any given time. It's one thing to file a letter; quite another to create and maintain a system for tracking inquiries, storing resource materials, recording project expenditures or maintaining a database system. What we are really talking about here is another major discretionary skill of the secretary: information-handling.

Telephone Skills. Answering the telephone is a big area that varies in degree of discretionary skill applied. Letting you know who's on the line is basic, so is keeping a running log of which calls need to be returned in the course of a day. But what about the secretary who is able to remember which people are connected to each account and how important such people and accounts are to you at any given moment? And isn't this secretary even more valuable if he or she has a knack for picking up this information without it having been specifically provided?

Then there's the whole area of taking messages in your absence or when you're busy on another line. A secretary must know not just how to take down a caller's name and number, but what questions to ask and how much or how little of the message you will need to know in order to follow through on the call. A secretary must not just answer the phone, but decide whether to interrupt you or how important it is to track you down to take the call or to deliver a message if you're not around.

One manager marveled at his assistant's ability to seemingly pull names and numbers out of a hat. Sometimes Mark would have only spoken to someone once and then months later would want to get in touch with that person, not even at that point remembering his or her exact name. He'd say to his secretary, Clarice, "Do you remember that guy who called—he was a friend of So-and-so and he worked for some kind of clothing company. . . ." And Clarice would go to a file where she routinely filed names and numbers of people who weren't listed in the regular files, and more often than not would come up with the correct name. Mark would often say, "How do you *do* that?!" Now that's a secretary who's really on her toes.

Secretaries are known for establishing and maintaining relationships that exist purely over the phone—with secretaries of other managers, colleagues, business associates and others on whose cooperation a manager relies in order to accomplish work goals. Considering the handicap the telephone can present in clear communication, a secretary's ability to develop these relationships for the benefit of a boss is no simple feat, relying heavily on a secretary's communication and interpersonal skills. For example, secretaries proficient in "telephone skills" can be invaluable in dealing with vendors who may have hundreds of accounts just like theirs, so that managers can come to expect prompt and immediate service just because the vendors have come to know the secretaries through whom business is conducted.

Discretionary telephone skills also include knowing what manner to use with different callers, presenting an appropriate image on the boss's behalf when placing or receiving calls. Now we're getting into one of the most important discretionary skills of the secretary: public relations.

Public Relations. Secretaries act as liaison between managers and all other people with whom they come into contact—both inside and outside the company. Secretaries must necessarily serve as ambassadors, setting the mood of new relationships and creating first impressions of the company and you. You probably rely on your assistant's public relations skills every day without even realizing it. You're a busy manager dealing with many people who all desire immediate attention. A secretary is your diplomat when you need a buffer between you and the rest of the world. A secretary is a client relations representative every time he or she answers the phone or greets someone who comes to call. What would you do without a secretary who knows how to coddle that difficult client and hold him off until you are able to attend to him? And what would it cost if that client got fed up with waiting and didn't have that soothing voice to calm his nerves while he impatiently waits for you to speak to him? And what about those who feel their call is crucial, even though you have five other "crucial" calls to return before you get to them?

Language/Communication/Interpersonal Skills. Basic grammar, spelling and a command of the English language are technical skills, yet there is a discretionary side to these as well. One secretary may be able to catch grammatical or spelling errors, and correct them. Another, however, may have the ability to grasp a manager's particular writing style and have a talent for drafting or editing your work in such a manner as to create documents the way you would have done it yourself—only you won't have had to take the time to do so.

Communication skills are in some ways technical, in terms of the ability to convey a message clearly both orally and in writing. But a secretary must not only relay information to and from a manager, but also gain the cooperation of others to accomplish work goals. Communication skills, combined with interpersonal skills, take on a discretionary flavor when it comes to using diplomacy, being persuasive or influencing others to act in a certain way on a boss's behalf.

Anticipating Needs. Secretaries make appointments and schedule meetings. But it's one thing to fill an opening in your appointment book and another to decide how much time a person will require or how much time you would want to set aside for a certain meeting, or to think about what times of day you prefer doing which activities or which times of day you like to keep clear. And it's one thing to set up a meeting, call participants and reserve a conference room. It's another to prepare the materials you will need for that meeting without having been told.

The Invisible Helping Hand

So far we've explored how typical support staff skills really serve a manager. Secretaries also do many things to keep the office afloat that very often go unrecognized. Such duties are often automatically performed by a secretary, assigned little importance, and tend to get taken for granted by the benefiting manager, while they in fact impact greatly on the accomplishment of a manager's work. It's a situation where no one stops to think about all that goes into the job while everything is going smoothly. But when the secretary isn't there for any reason, things fall apart.

Let's talk for a moment about one disorganized manager, Susan, as an example. Papers tend to fly when Susan is around. Her desk, and entire office, look as if a tornado hit. Yet, whenever Susan is looking for a certain file or document, her secretary, Marcia, always seems able to come up with it. What's happening is that while Susan never calls Marcia in and says, "Here are some papers that should be filed," Marcia takes it upon herself to go into Susan's office periodically to peruse the various piles of paper and organize them. She sorts which documents and files relate to matters that are not currently active (i.e., needed for the last day or two) and puts them where they belong. Marcia laughs to herself whenever she hears another manager marvel at how organized Susan is in spite of how disorganized she appears to be. What's ironic is that Susan herself is unaware of just how the system works; she only knows that it does. This is just one example of organizational skills in action.

Many a manager is totally unaware of the many things a secretary does routinely that not only save the manager time, but also reflect well on him or her. This is especially true in service industries where clients are involved. As Diane, a legal secretary, relates, "Clients call and ask for copies of things, or for non-work-related items, such as recommendations for a restaurant or hotel, for reservations to be made, or just to ask whether we know someone to contact here or there. There's often no need to tell my boss who called and what they asked for. I just do it."

Managers routinely send out packages that are extremely important and/or time-dependent. Many assume once a parcel is out of their hands, urgent documents will reach their destination, relying on a secretary to choose the best method of delivery. What they don't realize is that the secretary closely followed the package's progress, following up, checking and double-checking to make sure the package not only arrived at the proper destination at the proper time, but that it ended up in the hands of the right individual. The secretary's follow-through function often gets taken for granted.

In serving as liaison between the manager and others, a secretary often gets results without the manager even knowing what's gone into the accomplishment. One boss, Fran, frequently

PROJECT LOG

Date	Name	Assignment	Time In	Due	Time Req'd.	Order/Done

MANAGER FACT SHEET

Name _____ Title _____
SSN# _____ Dept. _____

Frequent flyer ID:
Airline _____ Number _____
_____   _____
_____   _____

Car rental ID:
Company _____ Number _____
_____   _____
_____   _____

Proper names, companies and affiliations frequently referenced:
_____   _____
_____   _____
_____   _____

Technical expressions, product descriptions, etc. frequently used:
_____   _____
_____   _____
_____   _____

Other important information: _____
_____
_____

TRAVEL ARRANGEMENTS REQUEST FORM

Name _____ Date Submitted _____
Day/Date of Departure _____
Destination(s)_____ Must Arrive By _____ am/pm
_____ (date/time)
_____ _____ am/pm
_____ _____ am/pm
Return From _____ Date _____ Time _____ am/pm
Air _____ First Class _____ Business Class _____ Coach _____
  To: (choice of airport) _____ Non-stop Only _____
Rail _____ Smoking _____ Non-Smoking _____ Window _____ Aisle _____
Hotel Preference _____ Special Requests _____
Car rental: Size _____ Options _____
Paying by: Cash _____ Credit Card _____ Check _____
VISA/MC/AE/OTHER _____ # _____ Exp. _____
Transportation needed to airport/terminal: Taxi _____ Car Service _____
Transfers needed from airport/terminal to hotel? Yes _____ No _____
Restaurant or other reservations needed: _____
  to include (names) _____
Passport/Visa needed for international travel to: _____
Cash advance required $_____
Other requests: _____

---

needed information from the Accounting Department during the interval between usual reporting periods. It was, of course, up to Sharon, Fran's secretary, to get this information. Jerry in Accounting was not easily approachable, since he had more than enough to do just to keep up with his regular work, let alone manually compile information for Fran whenever she wasn't willing to wait for the monthly computer printout. Sharon worked hard to develop a relationship with Jerry so that he would cooperate with Fran's frequent requests. Sharon traded favors and offered to help in any way she could to smooth over Jerry's ruffled feathers. It was true that Jerry really had no choice but to comply, since Fran was his ultimate superior, but through Sharon's efforts, his cooperation was more readily forthcoming.

A Job's Particulars—and a Support Professional's Special Talents

Secretaries also perform more specialized skills depending on the office, such as financial management skills—routinely working on budgets, client billing, accounts payable or receivable, payroll, tracking of expense accounts or getting involved in negotiating, calculating and controlling and reducing expenses. Secretaries often get actively involved in sales and marketing and are called upon to promote company products or services, actively sell, or answer inquiries. As more and more offices become updated and automated, secretaries are being called upon to research and select the equipment most appropriate for a company's needs. How a secretary actually contributes in an organization is largely dependent on what is needed by that organization. Since the secretary's job is so often officially unstructured, secretaries often just do whatever is necessary—filling the gap, so to speak—and that requires the input of each particular secretary's special talents.

Carolyn was secretary to a vice president, Anne, in a management consulting firm. This vice president's job was to write proposals, sell training programs, create such programs and then conduct the actual training. Anne's forte was clearly in the selling phase of this cycle, her persuasive proposals only topped by her dynamite presentations. But when it came to writing the actual training program, Anne was less enthusiastic—training just didn't hold the same challenge as selling.

Anne found, to her pleasure, that Carolyn was extremely interested in program development. Not only did she enjoy researching information to be included in programs, she really had a knack for putting together highly appealing participant training manuals. Since the training manual itself—to be kept by the client—was a major portion of the product, this talent turned out to be extremely helpful in ensuring a satisfied client. Anne and Carolyn were a team: Carolyn delivered to the client what Anne promised.

The benefits didn't stop there, either. Carolyn was so motivated by contributing to the team effort that her other duties were accomplished in record time. Anne seized upon every opportunity to capitalize on Carolyn's apparent creative talent, for instance, asking her to design an advertisement for the company's entry in a convention directory, and including her in the creation of a new company promotional brochure. Not only was Carolyn motivated by such assignments, but the company won also by saving money.

You may ask the question, at what point does a Carolyn begin to ask for a promotion or more money? Certainly, at some point he or she will—and should. A person should be recognized and compensated for the value of his or her contribution. We'll cover that in Chapter 5.

Management Skills in Disguise

Many people think, "A secretary is a secretary is a secretary." And along with this line of thinking goes the belief that secretaries are not, nor could they ever be, managers. The truth is that many skills of the secretary are in fact management skills utilized on a different level.

Planning is a basic management skill. Secretaries plan too. A secretary must plan how to get work done on time by organizing a workload and determining priorities. Managers coordinate; secretaries also use coordination skills in accomplishing assignments by juggling time, people and tasks, in spite of constant interruptions of people and the telephone. They coordinate their workload according to availability of equipment, where sharing is required, for instance, working around peak times at the copier. Coordination also requires effective time management—well accepted as a valuable managerial skill.

Secretaries are not often thought of as decision-makers, and it's true that historically secretaries have not been empowered to make many decisions of bottom-line importance. But a secretary does make decisions every day, even though they are of a different nature than those of top executives. The decision-making process, however, is the same regardless of what the decision is, and a competent secretary needs a grasp on the process to be successful, just as an executive does. Support professionals use decision-making daily, especially in connection with the handling of information in addition to prioritizing, organizing their workload, screening telephone calls and handling matters in the boss's absence.

Another key managerial skill of the secretary is problem-solving. Secretaries routinely use problem-solving in connection with office administration and procedures, yet the skills involved in identifying and finding solutions for problems in this area are easily transferable to other work situations. And, as has been discussed at length, secretaries regularly exercise interpersonal and communication skills in the daily accomplishment of their work.

So what is the secretary's role on the management team? That role should not be prejudged and cannot be generalized. Your secretary's function should fit your specific situation. Within your organization and department, your secretary should do whatever is necessary to best accomplish the secretary's purpose—that is, to provide you with professional support in getting the job done. Don't be boxed in by assumptions of what a secretary does. Continually look for ways to expand what your secretary can do for you.

By now you should realize that secretaries are not all alike and that few resemble the outdated stereotype. Look at your support position and your secretary or assistant as unique. They are. Learn to make the most of your secretary's function and the special talents he or she brings to the job.

The Role of Support Staff in the 1990's and Beyond

Today's office support professional has come out from behind the scenes to make significant, direct contributions to accomplishing a manager's and organization's goals. It's support staff who are most comfortable with advanced technology and who should take an active role in choosing the equipment that meets a company's needs, as well as train people to use it. While support staff have always been troubleshooters, they should now be encouraged to become true problem-solvers: to identify situations that need correcting and to suggest alternative solutions. Handling information is traditionally central to the support staff role. From here on, support staff must be true "information managers" and "answer finders": highly involved in ensuring that managers have immediate access to the information they need to meet objectives. Support staff must continue to evolve to meet the quickly changing business environment: support professionals should be proactive at the forefront of change rather than sit back and wait for its effect.

MAKING IT WORK

There's a saying to the effect that if you take care of the little things, the big things will take care of themselves. This philosophy can be adapted to the secretary/manager relationship. If the basics are in place, the environment will be ripe for development of a truly effective work team. Let's build a solid foundation and work our way up to loftier ideals.

In the ideal secretary/manager situation, the two work "in sync" with one another. Working as a team requires coordination of effort. You start by getting organized.

Getting Organized

Remember the old saying, "A place for everything and everything in its place"? You and your assistant should establish where to keep things you might need from each other. Set aside a special place for current files and working papers, whether it be a drawer of your credenza or just a corner of your desktop. Very often a secretary needs certain information while working on a document—perhaps the address of someone or the spelling of a name—that can be found in your working papers. It's more efficient for your assistant to find needed information on his or her own than to interrupt you or wait until you're available to ask you the question. (See page 75 for sample "Manager Fact Sheet," which will contain information needed frequently by your support staff.)

Also think of the things you might need: general supplies, such as folders, note pads, pens and pencils, petty cash slips or other procedural forms. It's good to be able to help yourself rather than do without because your assistant is out to lunch or too busy working on a project to find something for you.

Support staff need to know where you keep your calendar and personal Rolodex file, if you have one. You need to know where your assistant keeps a Rolodex and how locally stored files are kept. You should also have a general idea of how to gain access to files that are not kept in your area should you need something in your secretary's absence.

Set up mutually comfortable systems of operation. First, consider paper handling. Most people use in and out boxes for intercompany mail; use the same system between the two of you so you need not interrupt one another every time you want to move something to the other's desk. Decide whether to use a separate box for filing and agree on how often it should be checked. Using a "to be filed" box is helpful in keeping your desk clear, if you're one of those people who tends toward clutter. If you're just not the type to be diligent about a clean desk, think about having your secretary check your desk periodically when you're not around to look for noncurrent items that may be filed.

Set up a system for recording names, addresses and phone numbers. If you maintain a Rolodex in your office, have your assistant routinely make up two cards each time a person is added. Let your assistant know of any special information you want included, such as a person's secretary's name, as well as just how you like the information recorded—phone number at the top right, and so on.

Set up a system for answering the telephone and placing your calls. Decide whether you will answer the phone yourself or have incoming calls screened. Keep in mind that continual interruptions to answer the phone or place a call are most disruptive to a secretary who is trying to get work accomplished. If you usually talk to almost everyone who calls after they have been announced, you should consider answering the phone yourself. Even if you answer the phone as a matter of course, you can still ask your secretary or assistant to pick up all calls when you are in a meeting or need to concentrate fully on a given project.

Let your secretary or assistant know just how you would like the phone answered, including the combination of information to be relayed to callers: your name, the secretary's name, the department, a greeting or question. Some examples:

- "Ms. Jones's office, Sara Smith speaking."
- "Audit, Sara Smith speaking."
- "Good morning, Ms. Jones's office."
- "Audit, Sara Smith speaking. How may I help you?"

If your phone is so busy that support staff must pick up overflow calls, decide whether you want a log of incoming calls kept in order to help you keep track of what calls you need to return in the course of a day or week and how much information should be recorded—name, number, time of call, subject, follow-up, etc.

Placing calls yourself is more efficient. If you do ask your secretary to place your calls, make it clear *in advance* what your secretary or assistant should say if the person you want to reach is not available: that the person should return the call, that you will call back later, or that you wish to leave a message. *Never* ask your secretary or assistant to place a call and then decide to squeeze in an errand. It's aggravating for a support professional to get someone on the line only to find out you've disappeared. It's generally not well received on the other end either.

Your secretary or assistant needs to know the names and relationships of people who are important to you and your work in order to make appropriate decisions when these people call: what to say, whether to interrupt you, what questions to ask, where to route the call in your absence. Don't expect support staff to instinctively know, although, as has been discussed in this chapter, some often do. Make it a point to provide that information as a matter of course. Provide a list of significant people, and update it periodically. Such a list is also helpful when your secretary or assistant is out for any reason and someone else fills in.

Choose a central location and device for keeping telephone messages in case your secretary or assistant is away from the desk when you are ready to return calls. Messages should be kept by your secretary until you are ready to handle them; if your secretary hands you a message every time a call comes in, you're bound to lose track of more than one. Here again a log can be helpful.

Setting Rules and Standards

Set out rules and expectations right from the start.

Hours of Work. Make support staff clearly aware of what all the implications of 9:00 to 5:00 are to you. If you expect your assistant not just in at 9:00 but ready to roll at 9:00 sharp and not 9:06, set this out from the start. If overtime without previous notice is the rule rather than the exception, your secretary or assistant must realize this from the start as well.

Be clear about lunch rules. Do you want your secretary to take a lunch hour at the same time you do, or would you rather have him or her cover the phones in your absence? How much flexibility will you allow for length of lunch hour or when lunch is taken? Will your secretary be expected to work through lunch occasionally or frequently—without prior notice?

What are your feelings about conducting personal business at the office, whether during work hours or not? How do you feel about personal phone calls? What about time off for personal business during work hours?

It's a good idea to get all expectations out in the open—but bear in mind that flexibility where possible is always well received and, handled prudently (within company guidelines), can serve as a basis for favor-trading when you need help above and beyond the call of duty.

Who Is Where? Rules should go both ways. Complaints are loud and frequent from both managers and secretaries that one often disappears without a word to the other. A good rule is that you will tell each other when you leave the work area. It's also helpful to include where you are going and when you expect to return. Even if you're just stepping away for minute, it's important to let your secretary know, because a minute can easily turn into 15 if something or someone sidetracks you along the way. You should, of course, always let your secretary know where you are or how you can be reached so a secretary can best handle callers in your absence. If you do not wish to reveal exactly where you are headed, you can at least provide a general direction so your secretary or assistant can track you down if need be. Support staff can be instructed to leave a message in an obvious place if called away from the desk for any reason, being sure to include the time and not just "I'll be back in 10 minutes."

When you're out of the office at meetings or traveling, set up rules for calling in periodically. If your secretary or assistant will be absent on a given day, insist on a call in plenty of time to arrange for coverage.

What's Off Limits. We talked earlier about knowing where to look for things in each other's work areas. You should also set up rules about areas in each of your offices where the other is not to venture, perhaps a locked desk or file drawer. Also, let your secretary or assistant know how you feel about others entering your office in your absence.

One secretary's experience illustrates how important this rule can be. Andrea's boss, Pat, was frequently out of the office and never said anything to Andrea about whether to allow staff members to go into her office in her absence. Andrea noticed Jacqueline, a manager of equal rank to Pat, entering Pat's office on two occasions when Pat was away. Since Pat had never instructed Andrea to keep people out of her office, Andrea was not sure how to handle this situation. On a third occasion, Jacqueline found Pat's office locked and asked Andrea for the key. Andrea refused to open the office. It was one thing to confront a superior about entering another superior's office, but it was quite something else to help that person through a locked door. Upon Pat's return, Andrea reported all three incidents to her boss. Andrea's instincts were right: Pat had noticed her desk had been rifled as a result of the first two incidents and so had locked her office this last time. From then on it was clear: no one was to enter the office except Andrea in Pat's absence.

Maybe you're not comfortable about even your secretary having access to your work space. If you want your desk and office left untouched in your absence, make that a rule as well.

Support Professionals Aren't Mind Readers. As will be more fully discussed in Chapter 4, many secretaries complain they don't know what is expected of them on the job. Be explicit in your demands. If when you call in from the road, you expect your secretary to be available and ready with a complete report, make that known so he or she can be prepared and won't choose to go out for lunch at the appointed time. If you want to be left completely alone for a certain time period each day, say so. If you expect your secretary to make sure you leave on time for appointments, ask for help. Support staff are there to assist you and can only effectively do so if you're clear about what you need. Don't leave things to chance!

Assigning Responsibility—and Authority

Speaking of not leaving things to chance, to avoid mistakes and reduce anxiety, set out clearly where responsibility lies. And, remember, in those cases where responsibility lies with your secretary, always delegate appropriate and sufficient authority to enable him or her to carry out such duties effectively and efficiently.

Scheduling. Decide who is to keep your calendar, make your appointments and where appointments are to be recorded. If you keep your own schedule on a calendar in your jacket, purse or briefcase, set up a system to keep your secretary or assistant abreast of your plans as far in advance as possible. If you use more than one calendar, designate one as the "official" schedule to which you may both refer to avoid scheduling conflicts. Whether or not your assistant is responsible for scheduling appointments, always tell your secretary when you make an appointment for yourself. Support staff are asked many times in the course of a day whether you are expected to be in on this morning or that afternoon—it helps to have the same information you do concerning your expected whereabouts at all times.

If you designate your secretary or assistant as responsible for keeping your calendar, also delegate and abide by his or her authority to make appointments for you. It's a waste of time to tell your secretary to set up a lunch meeting for you and then for the secretary to go back and forth between you and the other parties to find an acceptable date. Either give your secretary the authority to pick a time and date based on your calendar or do it yourself.

Travel. The same thing goes with making travel arrangements. If your secretary is responsible for your travel plans, make clear your needs and wishes in advance and then give your secretary the authority to make choices for you (see "Travel Arrangements Request Form" on page 76). It's frustrating and a waste of valuable time for your secretary to run back to you with all the options available for your decision. Give enough information in advance so your secretary can make intelligent decisions on your behalf. In addition to the date of departure and return, what support staff need to know:

- Your travel time preferences—time you want to leave no later than, time you must arrive by.
- Whether you are traveling alone.
- Your desired class of service and seat preference—smoking or nonsmoking, aisle or window.
- Choice of airport (some cities have more than one)—whether you insist on nonstop or don't mind stopovers.
- How you will pay, whether by check or credit card, and your credit card number.
- Whether tickets will be picked up or mailed.
- Whether you will need a car—preferred size, special options and so on.
- Accommodations required—hotel preference and type of room.
- Your desired method of transfer from arrival point to hotel or other destination.
- The amount of travel advance you will require.

Ordering Supplies. Your secretary should handle supplies ordering completely, including shopping around for the best materials at the best price. Here, again, delegate the authority for your secretary to carry out this task; give your secretary parameters to work within and allow the secretary to make the decisions. It's inefficient if an order cannot be placed until you have approved it, and you're too busy to do so for days or weeks. And it's aggravating to go to the supply closet to find the cupboard bare because you weren't available to approve an order.

In Your Absence. Many secretaries routinely hold the fort when their manager is away, yet complain their efforts are stymied because they don't have the authority to make practical decisions. Handled on a case-by-case basis, the wise delegation of authority in your absence can best keep the office running smoothly even when you're not there. Don't leave things to chance when you're away. Clearly set out what matters your secretary should handle (giving express authority for him or her to do so), what matters can wait until your return and what matters require your handling from afar.

Establishing a Routine

The vast majority of secretaries and managers work together haphazardly: managers assign work as it arises; their secretaries have no real direction, just move from one project to another as priorities shift. It's inefficient and even counterproductive for a manager to call a secretary in or go out to a secretary every time he or she thinks of something for the secretary to do. It's much more effective and better received by a secretary to work with a plan.

Regularly meet with your secretary or assistant to plan upcoming work activities and to monitor progress on ongoing projects. A routine meeting each morning to discuss what's to be done that day sets the stage for a productive day. Regular weekly meetings to outline the status of projects provides a solid basis for decision-making concerning work priorities by your secretary. These meetings should not be catch-as-catch-can; rather, they should fill a regular slot on your calendar.

A secretary or assistant can only work on one project at a time, and works best without constant interruptions—just as you do. Except in cases of high priority, curb the impulse to give support staff new assignments as they occur to you, and have your secretary refrain from running in to you for a signature every time a letter is ready to be mailed out. Instead, meet with your secretary or assistant periodically to exchange what you need from one another, perhaps right before lunch or during the last hour of the day.

When You Share a Secretary

The reality is that most managers must share support staff with one or more other managers or staff members. In this case, it is even more important that you develop a good relationship with the secretary since you will in effect be competing with others for the secretary's help.

If it is your secretary's designated responsibility to keep a senior manager happy above all others, you must first make sure your relationship with the secretary is such that he or she will at least do as much for you as humanly possible. If the secretary's best is still not enough, you may have to rely on the good will of other secretaries in the office to fill the gap. The keys to success in this case are maximum consideration and large doses of appreciation for help received.

In most other situations, work should be completed by the secretary in terms of priority. Number one, be honest about the priority of your work. You won't win any points with a secretary if you're always pushing for your work to get completed first regardless of its urgency. When conflicts arise over whose work is more urgent, don't put support staff in the middle; confront the involved manager directly and settle the matter between yourselves.

When asking a support professional for what amounts to a favor—whether you're asking your own secretary to put your work ahead of someone else's or if you're asking another secretary to help you out—*never* make your request a demand. Always remember the old saying about catching more flies with honey—overbearance will certainly move your work to the bottom of the pile if it gets added to the pile at all.

Some support staff tend to complete work for the highest-ranking boss first, regardless of priority, or for the manager with whom the secretary or assistant shares the best relationship. If you're the lucky manager, you may be tempted to leave it at that. However, in fairness to all, remember how it feels to be on the short end of the stick and encourage support staff to consider everyone's needs and not just your own. The best way around this situation is to develop a system for keeping track of work assignments. A log can be used to record work assignment, assigning manager, estimated time needed for completion and due date (see sample "Project Log" on page 74). The log keeps the secretary from showing favoritism and neutral in cases of conflict while providing a basis for settling disputes.

Regular meetings should be held between support staff and managers as a work unit. At such meetings, managers can share anticipated work needs for the coming week, two weeks, etc., and the group can work out a tentative plan for meeting everyone's needs. It also helps to have support staff attend regular staff meetings to gain a clear understanding of how each individual's projects fit into the total department picture. You should also meet on a one-on-one basis with your secretary or assistant to keep the relationship on an even keel, to clear up problem situations before they grow out of control and to find creative ways for your secretary or assistant to contribute to the accomplishment of your work goals.

If you experience periods when your work isn't getting done because support staff are overly burdened, look into the possibility of hiring a temporary secretary to help with the overflow. If your secretary or assistant is seriously overextended on a regular basis, it's time to prove the need for more help. A well-documented appeal may convince upper management to hire another person, perhaps at least on a part-time basis.

If it's accepted that support staff are indeed overburdened, yet no relief can be granted due to budgetary or other considerations, make an extra effort to ease the stress created by the workload. Simple acts of consideration will go a long way. Offer to do your own copying and collating when possible, for instance. Invite your secretary to lunch or offer to bring a soda or cup of coffee to break up the day. Above all, take a few minutes out of your own busy schedule to talk to your secretary about how the work is going. Sometimes just having someone to listen about how difficult it is to keep up with the work is all a secretary needs to catch a second wind.

GETTING THE MOST FROM THE SUPPORT STAFF/ MANAGER RELATIONSHIP

You will gain the most benefit from working with support staff if you recognize that support staff are key members of your team.

A Model for Support Staff/Manager Teamwork

A client once observed that support staff and managers work together along a continuum. One end of the continuum represents tasks that, presumably, only support staff can do. The other end represents tasks that, again presumably, only the manager can do. This client believed that the ability of support staff to move toward the right of the continuum depends on what she called the principle of "sequential trust." This means that before proceeding to higher-level tasks, support staff must first prove they are competent in areas for which they are already responsible.

Susan Marc Lawley, a partner in my firm, StepTakers, and I have built on this observation to develop the Support Staff/Manager Teamwork Model (pictured on page 90). The left side of the model represents the support staff end of the continuum; the right side, the manager end. There is a gray area of overlap in the center that is, in effect, up for grabs. We suggest that managers and support staff should actively negotiate to determine what goes on in that gray area to the team's best advantage.

We believe that the size of the gray area and how far it will move to the right or left in a given situation depends on several factors. First is the skill level of the support person in question and how well the manager utilizes such skills. The manager's perspective of the support role is key in this process. If a manager fails to see support staff as key team members, the gray area will shrink and move to the left regardless of the secretary's skills and abilities.

A secretary's motivational level and ability to communicate expectations and goals to the manager then come into play. We commonly find support staff who feel underutilized and who have the ability to take on more responsibility, but who have not let their managers know that they want to do more. A manager must also be approachable and open to hearing support staff ideas. The question then is how willing is a manager to delegate. Ego comes into play: Is the manager comfortable sharing what may be considered managerial duties? Situations also arise where support staff have the skills and managers want to delegate more challenging work, but the support professionals in question don't believe there will be a reward for taking on the extra responsibility. A secretary must believe there's something in it for him or her to take on higher level work.

The seniority of the manager determines his or her ability to

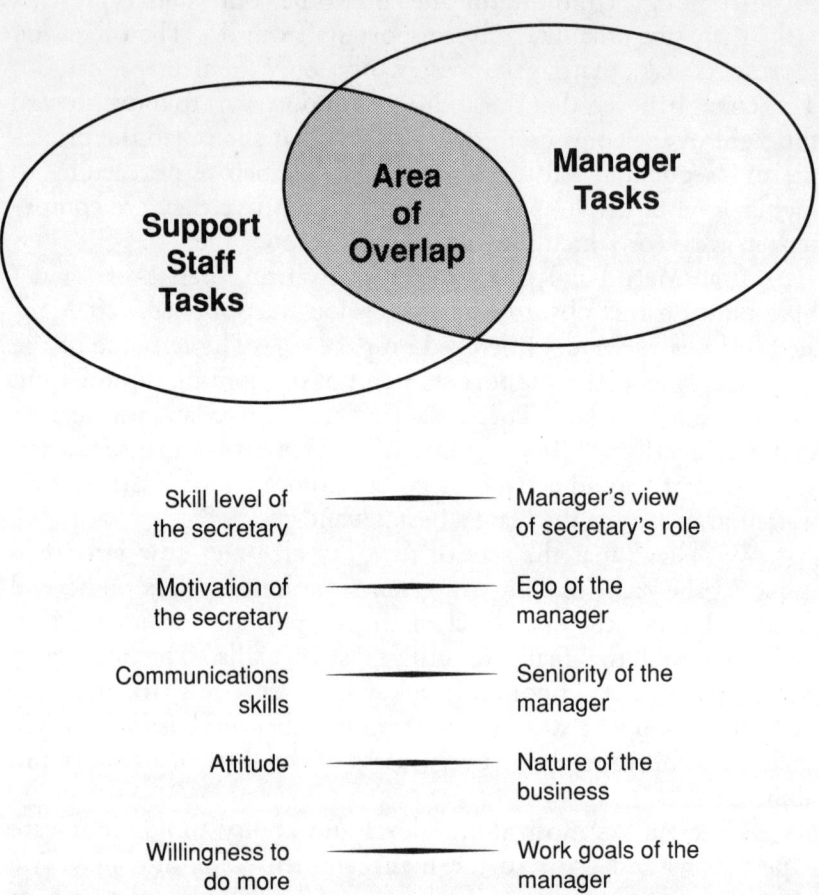

pass on authority to support staff to carry out delegated responsibilities. To move the gray area to the right, a support professional must possess a positive attitude and be willing to take on additional responsibilities. Even with all of these variables in line, many a support professional still remains frustrated because a manager continues to handle things a secretary may be willing and able to do. At this point, the manager's goals, the nature of the client's business and the people he or she serves may be behind the choice not to delegate.

For example, we heard the story of a secretary who complained that her manager scheduled his own appointments rather than allowing her to do so. The secretary felt that this was rightly within her purview. Surmising the manager didn't trust her ability to handle that task, she took affront. What came to light was that their department was responsible for bringing new business into the firm. The manager's goal was to court prospective clients and persuade them to allow the company to handle their financial affairs. At the outset, the personal touch was critical in establishing a relationship with the potential client. Once the new client was on board, it was the manager's further goal to get to know the client, to identify their style, likes and dislikes. Placing the phone call to schedule appointments then gave the manager an opportunity to make casual conversation with prospective clients, to get to know them better.

We often find that when there is tension in a given work relationship, it can often be diagnosed using this model. Sometimes it is not clear whether secretary or manager is responsible for performing a task that falls within the gray area. Efforts may be duplicated, creating mutual frustration, or, worse, important tasks may slip through the cracks causing manager and secretary to miss deadlines or not achieve goals. Or there may be disagreement over how tasks within the gray area are assigned, as in the case cited above. In this situation, team members should review the factors listed below the model to find a rationale for changing responsibility or for keeping the status quo. The model provides a basis for meaningful communication that can resolve the tension. As for the secretary who wasn't scheduling appointments, once she understood the reasons for the manager's actions, she no longer felt insulted and the two went on to identify other ways in which the secretary could help achieve those same goals.

Following this model, utilize the full range of your secretary or assistant's skills and abilities as they relate to your secretary's and your own goals, as well as those of your department and company.

Your Information Manager

Here are some of the things a secretary can do with information:

- Analyze it.
- Compile, control, convey, condense it.

- Distribute, deliver, evaluate, expand it.
- Obtain, organize, process, present it.
- Research, review, record, retrieve it.
- Study, summarize, supply, store it.
- Translate it.

Take advantage of the support staff vantage point and involve your secretary or assistant in the information-processing aspects of your work to save time and improve efficiency.

Do not have your secretary or assistant just open the mail, but prepare it to provide you with instant access to what you need to know. Your secretary can peruse, sift, sort and prioritize, screen, summarize and comment on incoming mail. If you routinely receive mounds of unsolicited mail, explain how you would like material handled—what pieces should be discarded, where others should be routed, and so on.

Common requests or inquiries requiring routine responses can be handled completely by support staff with proper instruction. If you receive lengthy journals, reports or other memoranda, have your secretary or assistant read and summarize them, highlight pertinent sections and perhaps prepare an abstract for you.

In short, don't limit support staff participation to mere paper-stacking; allow your secretary or assistant to get involved and exercise intelligence in actually helping you process the enormous amounts of information you must deal with in your work.

Information-handling should not be limited to that which is on paper, either. Information travels by telephone and through the people with whom you, and your secretary on your behalf, come into contact. Do not have your secretary or assistant just answer the phone or relay messages between you and others, but keep records of contacts, relationships and progress of projects.

Your Eyes and Ears

So much for the practical aspects of information-handling. In the role of communications link between you and others, support staff can effectively function as your eyes and ears. You can't be in all places at all times; indeed, you are often busy behind closed doors or on the road conducting business. If you do not benefit from your secretary's perceptual skills, you exist in isolation.

Support staff are privy to a realm of information above and beyond official meetings and memos that otherwise keep you informed. Even if you're on the grapevine, support staff have access to a different perspective of what's going on in an organization: a secretary who is a link in the information communication chain of a company has her finger on the pulse of that organization. You can find out, for example, how others reacted to your ideas at a meeting, who's gunning for your job, who's looking for another job, who's maligning you or who's admiring you. If you're not tapping into this powerful information source, you're losing out on invaluable help.

One manager, Henry, routinely relied on his secretary's exercise of what he dubbed "prudent power." Henry used this term to describe how his secretary, Devan, influenced his actions by sharing with Henry her thoughts and ideas about goings-on in the office, politically, and work-wise as well as by providing him with information he might not otherwise come by. He called this influence "prudent" because Devan was always careful not to be overly pushy in expressing her opinions, and, indeed, according to Devan, was careful always to express her respect for Henry's authority.

Henry finds that Devan's access to information and personal insights often provide missing pieces to Henry in solving many everyday work puzzles. In one case, Henry needed to replace a key manager in his department. Very particular about new hires, Henry spent six months choosing the new manager. Soon thereafter, it was clear the manager was not going to work out. As Henry discussed the situation with Devan, she shared her ideas concerning someone already on staff who she thought was a strong candidate for the position. Devan's suggestion was based on her solid knowledge of what Henry sought in a manager, having worked for him for several years, and in seeing in this staff member just the qualities she thought would fit Henry's requirements. Although the matter was never discussed again, the staff member in question was in fact promoted to the manager slot. While Devan doesn't feel entirely responsible for the promotion, she does believe her contribution had some impact on how Henry saw the situation.

In another instance, Devan's grapevine connections provided Henry with information that saved the department from a serious potential problem. Devan heard that the company's credit union was making plans to move into the space directly adjacent to Henry's department, Internal Audit. Since the effectiveness of Internal Audit requires that the department remain detached from other company departments, confidentiality of its operations is crucial. This confidentiality could certainly be compromised if a credit union were operating right next door, with people coming and going by the department all day. With Devan's advance warning, Henry was able to stop the planned move before it took place.

DELEGATING TO SUPPORT STAFF

We've talked specifically about how support staff can help you manage information. Now let's take a broader look at the issue of delegating and hear some examples of sequential trust in action. It has been estimated that managers spend an average of 53% of their time performing tasks that could be handled by support staff. Examine your work habits and determine where delegation is in order.

Diane, a legal secretary, tells how attorneys often waste valuable time on client billing by merely relying on their secretaries to do the typing involved. Diane's boss, on the other hand, has her handle complete billing preparation, from gathering and double-checking fee and expense figures, preparing activity descriptions, putting everything into proper billing format to writing cover letters. Ed has only to review the bills, if he so desires, and sign the letters. Of course, Diane did not take on the entire task overnight; she was first required to prove her ability by drafting bills for Ed's approval. When it became clear she didn't need Ed's input, Diane was given full responsibility, including handling any follow-up inquiries clients might have.

As secretary to the Director of Corporation Communications of a large corporation, Kathy was as surprised as her manager, Tim, to discover skills she possessed that, as she put it, "I didn't realize were things everyone couldn't do." Tim handled speechwriting for top company executives. As Kathy typed the speeches, she found it made sense to arrange copy according to phrasing rhythm and natural breaking points. Picking up on Kathy's apparent talent, after the first couple of instances Tim gave her free reign in speech setup, leaving Tim to concentrate on the words themselves. Kathy's efforts proved extremely helpful to speakers, and the quality of the finished product reflected well on both Kathy and Tim.

Kathy's talents appeared in other areas as well. Public Affairs regularly put out a "daily news briefing" which consisted of news clippings of interest to company employees. In her work with electronic databases, Kathy found a way to access a synopsis of daily news highlights on international, economic and domestic levels. She then figured out how to transfer the summary from the database into her word processing system, where she formatted it to be combined with the other news clips. Kathy's talents in moving in and around the databases and computer equipment greatly increased the value of the daily news briefing—she was in effect publishing a daily newspaper for employees.

Joyce was executive secretary to the Vice President of Economic Research in a large corporation. Steven's work involved extensive use of visual aids—graphs and charts on 30-by-40-inch poster board and flip charts—for both in-house meetings and client presentations. Steven would show work in progress to Joyce and ask how it impacted on her and suggestions for improvements. Finding Joyce's input valuable, Steven began to ask her help in the actual preparation of graphics, a little at a time. As it became clear Joyce could handle entire projects on her own, Steven just made the assignment and left Joyce to her own design, so to speak. Joyce went on to take courses in graphics, and when Steven retired and was replaced by a woman with no artistic talent whatsoever, Joyce took over full graphics responsibility for the department.

Be secure enough to delegate to your secretary or assistant. You have nothing to lose and everything to gain: more valuable use of your time, increased team productivity, and perhaps a more satisfied assistant. A support professional's special talents will unfold only as opportunities are provided for them to be displayed and developed. Invite support staff suggestions on your project work and find ways to tap your secretary or assistant's creativity. For more ideas as to what new tasks you might delegate, look over and discuss the "Manager Needs" list on pages 36–37 in Chapter 2 with your secretary or assistant.

Fostering Growth and Encouraging Creativity

Be open to suggestions on your work. Expressing an interest in a support professional's suggestions will stimulate more ideas and inspire your secretary to find more ways to help you. If an idea is good, say so; if a suggestion won't work, use tact in explaining why so support staff can benefit from your knowledge and experience.

As you uncover potential, help in support staff development

by encouraging and, if possible, offering appropriate training. Look into available training within the company from which your secretary could benefit, or gather information on outside training programs to pass along to support staff. Training not only promotes professional growth, but is a proven motivator, and, as will be discussed in Chapter 5, can be used as a valuable perk for your secretary. A side benefit for you, as catalyst, is the pride you will experience as you see your secretary grow.

Building Trust and Cultivating Loyalty

Support staff are loyal to managers who are worthy of respect and who, in turn, respect support staff. High on the list of admirable qualities in a manager are honesty, integrity, intelligence, diligence, and loyalty to subordinates. Support professionals agree that respect must be earned, not demanded. Support staff respect managers who treat others, including support staff, as equal human beings. As one secretary puts it, nothing kills loyalty like a "peel-me-a-grape" attitude.

Support staff are loyal to managers who exhibit trust. Dare to confide. A secretary takes pride in what that title means: keeper of secrets. Start by conveying your belief in the importance of confidentiality and share tidbits of information. As your support staff proves worthy, take them further into your confidence.

Allow your secretary or assistant to exercise judgment and prove he or she is capable of handling work assignments, managing time and meeting deadlines without your intervention. Curb the impulse to get involved in every situation—give support staff room to handle responsibilities without overly close guidance or assistance. Give the benefit of the doubt. If your secretary doesn't appear as busy as you would expect, or seems to be on the phone too much, don't jump to conclusions. Everyone has their own way of completing work assignments—what should matter is results.

Support staff are loyal to managers who are trustworthy. Support staff learn to trust a manager whose behavior is consistent with his or her words—in matters most small to those of great significance. Support staff learn to trust managers who stand behind employees, who don't use people as scapegoats and who back up staff members when the need arises.

Support staff are loyal to managers who show consideration for support staff needs. If your secretary or assistant attends evening classes, don't ask him or her to work overtime on school nights. If he or she needs to catch a certain bus or train, take care not to cause him to miss it. Gail's experience is instructive. Tim understood that Gail required advanced notice to make child care arrangements in order to work overtime. Once arrangements were made, she could stay as late as necessary and often did work until nine, ten or eleven o'clock—until the job was done.

EFFECTIVE TEAMWORK IN ACTION

We have discussed many factors that contribute to the effectiveness of your support staff/manager team. Here are some tips in summary.

Tips for Increasing Support Staff/Manager Team Effectiveness

- *Work with goals and objectives.* Support staff need to be aware of a manager's, department's and company's goals in order to best manage time and direct work efforts. Office support professionals should also have their *own* career and work goals and share them with a manager to help determine areas for expanding support staff contribution.
- *Share expectations.* Both manager and support professional bring to the job preconceived ideas about the support staff role, what work is to be done and methods to use, how long assignments should take to complete, what comprises standard levels of performance and what the future will hold. Discuss these items with each other.
- *Define support staff responsibilities.* Role clarity is key to support staff effectiveness. Identify manager needs and support staff skills, agree on tasks and responsibilities that make best use of available time and each team member's strengths. Most importantly, look beyond traditional "secretarial" duties in deciding how your secretary or assistant can best help you achieve goals and objectives.
- *Maximize support staff contribution.* Utilize and develop the full range of support staff skills. Be open to input and delegate where appropriate. Also, have your secretary or assistant delegate those tasks that can be handled by less-

skilled staff members. Cast yourself in the role of instructor and teacher and identify ways for your secretary or assistant to grow in the job.
- *Coordinate time management efforts.* Meet regularly with support staff to discuss priorities, deadlines and changes in such. Minimize interruptions on both parts and avoid procrastinating. Find ways to move work smoothly from your office to your secretary's or assistant's work space and back again with a minimum of disruption to either's workday.
- *Eliminate environmental roadblocks.* See that available equipment and support services (copying, telecommunications, mail, etc.) are adequate for carrying out assignments. Question company policies and procedures that seem to hinder support staff's ability to get the job done. Determine whether your secretary or assistant's workload is sensible. Make the work environment as comfortable as possible.
- *Keep the lines of communication open.* Finding time and making the effort to talk to one another is probably the most important task of support staff and managers in building and maintaining a successful team. The next chapter will fully discuss all aspects of support staff/manager communication.

Complete the "Support Staff/Manager Teamwork Quiz" below to see how your team measures up in these areas.

SUPPORT STAFF/MANAGER TEAMWORK QUIZ

Consider how accurately each of the following statements reflects your *usual* experience. Circle "TRUE" if the statement is *always or almost always* true; circle "FALSE" if the statement is true only some of the time, seldom or not at all. Ask your secretary or assistant to independently answer the same questions and compare results. If there are differences, discuss how you might improve your team effectiveness.

	TRUE	FALSE
1. My assistant is aware of my goals and objectives as well as those of our department/company.	☐	☐
2. My assistant knows what is expected of him/her on this job.	☐	☐
3. I know what my assistant expects of this job.	☐	☐
4. My assistant and I regularly meet to discuss work priorities.	☐	☐

	TRUE	FALSE
5. My assistant feels free to ask me questions when my directions are unclear.	☐	☐
6. My assistant knows whether I am pleased with his/her work.	☐	☐
7. My assistant and I refrain from interrupting each other unnecessarily.	☐	☐
8. I am open to my assistant's ideas, opinions and suggestions.	☐	☐
9. My assistant regularly handles routine matters on my behalf.	☐	☐
10. My assistant has the help he/she needs to get the job done.	☐	☐
11. My assistant and I follow agreed-upon procedures to maximize our efficiency.	☐	☐
12. I delegate work that takes full advantage of my assistant's skills and abilities.	☐	☐
13. I give assignments to my assistant in plenty of time for their completion.	☐	☐
14. I let my assistant know how decisions that involve him or her have been made.	☐	☐
15. My assistant knows where to find me at all times.	☐	☐
16. My assistant has the equipment and support services needed to effectively complete work assignments.	☐	☐
17. My assistant is a true part of the team.	☐	☐

COMMUNICATION: The Key to Teamwork

Consider the following statistics from a survey of 4,000 secretaries conducted in 1986 by Panasonic Industrial Company and Professional Secretaries International:

- Seventy percent experienced a lack of communication with their supervisor.
- Nearly half felt inadequately informed on their firm's overall objectives and the goals of their own work.
- Thirty-eight percent complained they don't know what's expected of them on the job.
- Fifty-three percent felt there should be better communication concerning work priorities.

These results certainly point to communication as a critical issue in the effectiveness and success of the support staff/manager relationship. The study, which focused on the causes of secretarial stress, revealed that lack of communication was the *fourth most stressful characteristic* of the secretary's job. You can be sure that this does not translate into productive and happy working situations.

Faulty communication between manager and support staff hurts their relationship in two ways: first, a secretary or assistant who is not fully and accurately informed can't work at maximum performance levels. A major support staff role is that of information processor. How can a support professional successfully fulfill this role if a manager doesn't provide the necessary information? Second, less than satisfactory communication patterns can be demoralizing to support staff. Not only is it extremely frustrating to work without required information, it can feed a sense of unimportance that then leads to discontent on a secretary's part.

As a manager, you must be concerned not only with providing support staff with everything they need to know to accomplish work goals, but also with your own overall communication style. Without consciously working on this crucial area of the team relationship, all other attempts at building and maintaining a productive, successful team will be wasted. Communicating effectively with support staff is not a difficult matter—but it does require more than remembering to say "Thank you."

Manager-to-support staff communication has many problem areas, and most manager/support staff teams experience difficulty in many, if not all, of them. Most complaints, however, are variations on a theme. The manager tends to overlook the secretary or assistant, failing to share enough information for the secretary to work most effectively. Support professionals also complain that whatever information is conveyed comes cherry-coated, as if managers don't expect support staff to understand.

Again, apply your perspective as a contemporary boss. Your overall communication style must show your regard for support staff as professionals and as members of your team. Here are some specific guidelines for a successful communication relationship with your secretary or assistant.

GUIDELINES FOR EFFECTIVE SUPPORT STAFF/MANAGER COMMUNICATION

Conveying Organizational and Departmental Goals

It's startling how many support professionals are totally in the dark about the goals and objectives of the very companies for which they work—nearly 50% of those responding to the survey we just cited. Whether it's merely an oversight or because someone in the upper ranks doesn't think secretaries need to know, the result is the same—support staff feel unconnected to the work they do. It's no wonder so many secretaries feel isolated. No one bothers to tell them just what it is they're supposed to be accomplishing by showing up at work every day.

Think about how many meetings you've attended to be reminded of your company or department goals. It's probably more than you'd care to count. If your company has forgotten to fill in support staff on the overall objectives of the organization, step in and fill that gap. Then make sure your secretary or assistant is fully aware of your departmental and your specific work goals as well. Communicate not just the content of goals, but also the importance of what it is you're doing, so that he or she can feel a pride in participating. Invite your secretary or assistant to meetings whenever possible. Don't assume what goes on is nothing support staff need to know.

The purpose of clarifying goals goes beyond engendering a sense of connectedness and building a team spirit. Knowing the overall strategy helps support staff to effectively prioritize and allocate time to given projects. An uninformed secretary can be a roadblock to success by spending too much precious time on one activity to the neglect of other more important ones.

As team members, support staff must not only know what the team is doing, but also their part in accomplishing goals. Make support staff aware of how they fit into the achieving team goals. Let your secretary or assistant know precisely what is expected of him or her. An informed secretary or assistant is your best ally.

Keeping Your Secretary Up to Date

If your work pace resembles white rapids more than a babbling brook, keep support staff current on up-to-the-minute changes in priority or they will drown in the undertow. Fill in your secretary and briefly explain why a situation has changed. Nothing is more aggravating than to be working on a super rush all day, knowing nothing about it other than it must go out today, only to find at 4:00 P.M. that it's no longer needed. The secretary feels like the manager is capriciously pulling strings. After repeated episodes, support staff will view the manager as the boy who cried wolf and conclude that nothing is really a super rush job and won't respond to emergencies.

A smart manager explains how his or her supervisor had asked for the super rush in a frenzy in the morning and then received an emergency call in the afternoon on a different matter that superseded the original rush. Now the secretary can commiserate with the manager about the lousy day they're all having rather than react as though he or she's the cause of it.

In addition to changes in priority, keep support staff informed on the progress of projects. Fill in your secretary or assistant on what's happening—especially the more interesting aspects of a project. When you go to a meeting, for example, don't just tell your secretary you're going to such and such a place at such and such a time. Tell why you're going and the purpose of the meeting. Don't assume support staff aren't interested, or, worse, wouldn't understand. You'd be surprised how much many support professionals pick up just from preparing documents.

Knowing more about a project than what is seen on papers that cross a desk makes work more meaningful, creates interest and motivates support staff to do an even better job in participating in that project, whatever that participation may entail. Further, support staff who are kept abreast of the status of projects are better able to anticipate a manager's needs. Knowing that you're tense because you're waiting for a call on a given project can help your secretary or assistant decide on a course of action during that day, for example. If your secretary is unaware of what you're experiencing, he or she may inadvertently add to your anxiety by bothering you with matters that are better left until later.

This is not to suggest that you spend hours on end sitting around gabbing with your secretary. It only takes a couple of seconds to pass along bits of information and will go a long way to further drawing your secretary or assistant in as a real part of the team.

Don't forget your secretary at the conclusion of a project, either. Support staff often complain about working long hours on a project and then not being directly informed of its outcome. Many a manager has made the mistake of receiving the call that a client accepted a proposal, for example, and running straight past the secretary's desk to share the good news with other managers. Share the good news, as well as the bad, with your secretary.

Giving Clear Directions

First, make sure your secretary or assistant is aware of all aspects of a project. You'll get much better results on individual assignments if he or she understands the larger picture. Remember to pass on the background of the project, the names and relationships of all those involved and other relevant information in case a question arises when you're not around. It's humiliating for a support professional to get an urgent call on a matter and not to have a clue as to how the caller can be assisted in your absence. A secretary put into such a position feels stupid and embarrassed—not to mention furious with the manager who created the situation.

Remember that descriptive terms such as "soon," "quickly," "right away" and so on mean different things to different people. "Later" to you might mean this afternoon; "later" to your secretary may well mean tomorrow. Be specific! If you mean "this afternoon," say just that. Further, don't throw papers at your secretary as you are running down the hall. This kind of behavior causes secretaries to throw up their hands before they begin.

There's a plaque some secretaries keep on their desk that laments, "There's never enough time to do it right, but there's always enough time to do it over." It only takes a few minutes to carefully explain exactly what you need and when. Time spent at the outset always saves time and aggravation later.

Don't try to do three things at once when giving directions. If you're explaining an assignment to your secretary at the same time that you're dialing the phone and looking for something on your desk, chances are your directions will be less than complete. Further, you'll miss your secretary's reaction to what you're explaining. Take the time to notice whether your secretary seems to understand your directions. Even if your secretary has questions, it's unlikely those questions will get asked if you appear too busy to take the time to answer. Time will be wasted, errors likely be made and your secretary will be frustrated to boot.

Giving Productive Feedback

Support staff need feedback on performance, both positive and negative. If there's something your secretary or assistant does particularly well, take the time to say so. If there's something he or she does that does not meet with your expectations or needs, you must share this too—no matter how small a detail it might seem.

Take Al, for instance. Al was very satisfied with his secretary, Jan, overall. In particular, she was great on the phone with clients: remembered their names, recognized their voices and knew what to say and what not to say to each about the status of their accounts. The only problem was that Jan routinely didn't pick up the phone until the third or fourth ring. Al felt anxious every time the phone rang that the client was waiting too long. It became an obsession. What to say to Jan?

As in all cases of giving feedback, when the message is negative, be sure to point out the positives as well so that the recipient of the information doesn't feel like a total failure. Al pointed out to Jan all of the ways in which she is terrific on the phone and how much he appreciated her talents in this area.

Al then said, "There's just *one* thing. Please make it a point to pick up the phone on the first ring if at all possible. It's helpful, and I believe considerate, to save even a few moments of the client's time. But, most importantly, a ringing phone is one of those things that just gets to me!"

Jan could argue that there's really no difference to a caller between hearing one ring or three. But since Al presented the situation as a pet peeve of his, Jan can neither argue nor take offense. Everyone is entitled to their idiosyncrasies!—especially the boss.

Giving regular feedback is extremely important to the success of your relationship and to motivating support staff. Remarks concerning performance should not be saved until an official yearly review. In order for feedback to be effective, it must be provided close to the behavior exhibited. In other words, if your secretary or assistant did a great job putting together your materials for an important meeting, don't wait until the next time you're assigning something to say, "You did such a great job on my last set of meeting notes, here's another set. I need it in 10 minutes." Afterthoughts are not generally well received; neither are perceived attempts at manipulation.

If you notice that a set of materials looks great, take the 30 seconds it takes to say so—on your way to the meeting or as you return. Also, be specific; for instance, "The chart you prepared really helped me make my point." Mere pats on the back are not enough. Support staff need to know their work has meaning—that their efforts make a difference in helping a manager accomplish goals.

Most importantly, reactions to support staff performance should be given directly to the person involved—not to others. Your secretary or assistant needs to know how you think things are going and needs to hear it from you in a timely manner.

Listening Effectively

The health of the communication relationship you share with support staff depends on your making an effort to listen carefully to what your secretary or assistant is telling you. I use the term "listening" broadly to mean that you should, in fact, "listen" with more than your ears. You must learn how to "read" your secretary's behavior not only to notice whether he or she understands directions you may be giving, but also to keep on top of whether all is well or if something may be awry between the two of you.

Here is a case in point. John, as a new program administrator in a training firm, experienced firsthand how important this rule is. John's boss, Suzanne, assigned a project to him and then called in her secretary, Jeanette, to instruct her to do the copying John required to complete the project. Jeanette smiled and said, "Sure, Suzanne," and left the room. However, upon leaving, Jeanette clearly revealed just how she felt about the assignment. She sighed deeply and her face fell just the slightest bit as she heard the assignment. And as she left the room, the smile, which had been noticeably tight in the first place, vanished, and her eyes were on the floor. John did not miss this reaction. Suzanne, however, was already caught up looking at something on her desk and missed the entire display.

Not wanting to make an enemy of Jeanette the first week on the job, John took it upon himself to make his own copies and to set things straight between the two of them. He learned that Jeanette was overloaded with priority projects herself and felt it was unfair of Suzanne to load her with John's "junk work." John certainly understood her position. Suzanne, however, was not a smart manager. By not taking the time to notice that things were not right with Jeanette, she allowed Jeanette's resentment to grow, inadvertently sabotaging her productivity.

You can't solve problems unless you are aware that something is wrong. Don't be oblivious to messages just because they are not blatantly obvious. Get to know your secretary's communication behavior and you will soon become adept at spotting irregularities that may reflect potential difficulties in your working relationship.

Pick up on all nonverbal messages—everything about your secretary's communication outside the words themselves. Then if you think you detect a disparity between what is being said and what is displayed, or if he or she says nothing at all, you can tactfully open the door to discussion.

Handling Conflict

There is a hard-and-fast rule about handling conflict in the support staff/manager relationship: talk to your secretary about your secretary. It's as simple as that.

Don't complain to your friends or the Personnel Department when something is wrong, talk to your secretary or assistant directly. A friend in Personnel often laments, "Why do they always come running to me whenever there's a problem? I can't understand why they can't just work it out between them." It's not as if most situations are so earth-shattering as to require outside arbitration.

For example, Tom's secretary, Maureen, was habitually 10 to 15 minutes late each morning. It was very important to Tom that Maureen be at her desk first thing in the morning to answer the phones during what was their busiest time. When Maureen was not there on time, Tom's day started off all wrong. Tom was angry with Maureen before she even arrived, and Maureen couldn't understand why. Tom, unhappy about the situation, went to Personnel to complain about Maureen.

Aside from her tardiness, Maureen happened to be one of the top secretaries in the company. She felt something was up with Tom, because he was acting strangely. Personnel called Maureen in for a talk. This didn't do much for Maureen's morale. She felt insulted by such a petty complaint, especially since she often stayed well past quitting time to tie things up before leaving. In her mind, everything balanced out. Maureen sat and stewed.

Not only did Tom fail to solve his problem, he created a bigger one. Maureen's attitude toward the job and the company soured a little. If Maureen suspected that Tom instigated the scolding, it would have been all the worse for him.

Had Tom gone directly to Maureen, we might have had a happy ending to this story. Assuming Maureen was a reasonable woman, Tom's explanation may well have made sense to her, neutralizing her reaction to the complaint as petty. Further, their relationship would remain intact without the interference of an outside party and would even be strengthened as a result.

Certainly this example is a fairly uncomplicated situation. The fact is, most annoyances are of this same caliber. Small frustrations pile up and grow. That's why it's so important to nip small irritations in the bud. In the case of more complex problems, it's still the best idea to talk directly to your secretary or assistant to see if the two of you can't come up with workable strategies for rectifying the situation.

Confrontation is never easy. But considering the consequences of avoidance, it remains the wisest choice. In broaching problem situations, the best tactic is to keep the mood light. Don't confront when you're angry, that will only stir up defenses. Get your point across and then allow your secretary to give his or her side of the story. Airing differences and then putting your heads together to seek solutions is a far better course than taking the problem to the outside.

You must also follow the converse of this rule: Encourage your secretary to talk to you about you. Put yourself on the line and find out what you do that drives him or her crazy. If your ego is strong enough to take it, following this rule will provide many benefits. Number one, you get solutions to problem situations. Number two, the support staff/manager relationship will be strengthened. Number three, if your secretary or assistant feels free to come to you, it will curb participation in nonproductive coffee klatch activities.

You remember the coffee klatch—it's where support staff who do not share good relationships with managers spend a lot of time complaining about them. It's where support staff get support for not cooperating with you. It's where poor attitudes are born and low standards of production are nurtured.

Inviting discussion, of course, requires the use of a nonthreatening tone and a careful choice of words. Something like "Carolyn, I have a feeling something is not quite right. Would you tell me what's up?" is an open expression of willingness to listen. On the other hand, "Carolyn, will you please stop moping around and tell me what's wrong" may well evoke a defensive response.

SUPPORT STAFF/MANAGER COMMUNICATION TRAPS

The communication behavior of some support professionals reflects some of the occupational hazards of what it has historically meant to be a secretary. Since it takes at least two to form communication patterns, unenlightened managers often unwittingly fall into traps that can interfere with team development and negatively affect the work relationship. Understanding how the same factors that influence the relationship in other ways sometimes affect communication styles can help you overcome the problems that might arise.

"Just a Secretary" Mind-set

Some support staff are intimidated when talking with managers. There is a subconscious feeling that being only a secretary means an individual somehow isn't as good as others within an organization. Such intimidation can turn into a fearful communication style. A secretary may withhold thoughts, questions, ideas and suggestions, concluding that anything to be mentioned is only something you would already have thought of, or if not, is just not valuable. If you don't understand how a secretary feels, or worse, if you share a "just a secretary" mind-set, you may wrongly assume your secretary has nothing to contribute. In this case, it's up to you to draw the secretary out.

On the other hand, you may have come up against support staff who represent the opposite extreme. True professionals are fiercely proud of their profession. On the whole, they feel good about themselves and their work. But they may be angry, either consciously or unconsciously, because they think *you* don't recognize their importance. In this case, "you" means not only you as an individual, but also "you" as a representative of management or the world in general. This can translate into defensive communication behavior. These secretaries can be hostile or ultrasensitive to any indication that a manager doesn't consider them professionals, or as equals.

It's up to you to recognize where defensiveness is coming from, to be sure you aren't unwittingly contributing to it, and to diffuse hostility before it destroys your relationship. Don't get caught up in hostile behavior—keep your cool. Get past defensive or hostile behavior by tactfully insisting your secretary explain rather than stew in silence so that solutions may be found to problem situations.

Underutilization and the Perception Gap

Another hazard of the average support staff position that can negatively affect a person's communication behavior is having little practice in taking risks. If you think about it, support staff often sit safely behind the scenes watching managers take all the chances. Many support professionals have been offered few, if any, opportunities to take risks in the normal course of day-to-day work, and therefore rarely experience the boost of self-confidence that flows from taking chances and succeeding. As a result, many support professionals are afraid of taking risks in general and do not trust their own instincts. It may seem a monumental risk to approach a manager directly, to be really open or to share ideas. Many secretaries simply lack the confidence to talk to managers as equals. This can translate not only into a fearful communication style, but a silent one as well.

Low levels of self-confidence among support staff can also be fed by a lack of understanding about the true nature of the secretary's function. As already mentioned, some secretaries don't have a clear understanding of how they really contribute to the operations of a department and overall organization. Obviously, a person has to know the value of his work in order to feel good about it.

You can help build support staff confidence by your commitment to a contemporary view and by expressing your appreciation of the secretary's value. If you sense a person is holding back, draw him or her out.

Stereotyped Roles

A very common communication problem among support staff is a general nonassertiveness. The reasons behind this communication style are more complex than might be readily apparent. Sometimes individual personality has something to do with nonassertiveness. It is also a throwback to a sexual stereotype of women that existed before the feminist movement, and, of course, it is still true that most support staff are women. While assertiveness training has been popular for a long time, training programs aimed at support staff are only now becoming widespread.

Experience has shown, however, that problems with assertiveness are not simply tied to the individual secretary, but rather have more to do with the overall support staff/manager relationship. Years ago, the secretary/manager relationship was governed by then-accepted dominant/submissive male/female roles, since it was generally true that managers were men and secretaries were women. While it's safe to say that society is moving away from applying specific roles to men and women, the effect of stereotyped roles still lingers in the support staff/manager relationship. Maybe it has something to do with the fact that the secretary is the subordinate—this surely doesn't make it any easier for the secretary to break out of the submissive role. One can be assertive without crossing the line into insubordination, though.

In any event, the assertiveness problem is connected to how the support staff role is perceived. In professional development workshops conducted by the author, participants share with one another how they would handle given problem situations at the office. A typical scenario involves the secretary taking on many added responsibilities and asking the manager for a change in title and a raise.

Initially, each participant is asked in a round-table discussion to explain to the group how he or she would handle the situation. Participants generally are authoritative and articulate in stating their case, and appear confident of their ability to persuade a manager to see their point of view.

Next, two volunteers are asked to role-play the situation, with one as manager and the other as secretary. As the role-playing begins, it is immediately apparent that there is a big difference in how the manager and secretary behave. The secretary speaks softly, slouches noticeably in the chair, does not maintain meaningful eye contact, displays nervous gestures and generally comes across as meek and fearful. The manager, on the other hand, sits tall and straight, speaks in a strong voice, is articulate, and also is noticeably impatient with the whining secretary.

Next, the volunteers switch roles. The meek and mild secretary suddenly becomes the assertive boss and vice versa. By now, the rest of the workshop participants are aching for the opportunity to show the others how to do it right. But most teams exhibit the same behavior.

The truth is that many secretaries' communication behavior reflects an unconscious acceptance of the submissive nature of the secretarial role. Not until actually faced with the audience's candid reaction to each participant's behavior does the participant see that it is true—secretaries themselves are influenced by an outdated perspective of their role.

Obviously, a secretary who is unconsciously trapped in the submissive role has a limited ability to contribute as a full-fledged member of the organizational team.

Recognize the potential influence of stereotyping on your secretary's communication style. Make it a point to look beyond superficial behaviors to discover what support staff are really like. Be careful not to unwittingly encourage support staff to maintain stereotypical behaviors. Speak to support staff as equals—don't be patronizing. Don't play into attempts to cast you in the dominant role—challenge support staff to think independently and to express personal views to you. Encourage support staff to rely on their own judgment rather than to depend on you for continual reassurance. Show your willingness to take the time to discuss what your secretary considers important.

Overall

It takes two people to form a communication pattern. If the communication behavior of one party is altered, the other cannot help but change too in order to reach a new equilibrium. If you take the initiative in ensuring that your communication style reflects a contemporary view of support staff, your secretary or assistant may well grow in response.

KEYS TO SUPPORT STAFF MOTIVATION AND SATISFACTION

WHAT DO SUPPORT PROFESSIONALS WANT?

Once you've hired top-notch assistants, the trick is to motivate them to peak performance and keep them on board. What does it take to keep support staff happy? Office support professionals basically want three things:

1. Participation as team members and recognition for their contribution.
2. Opportunity for career advancement.
3. Compensation appropriate to their contribution.

All three are critical, yet compensation is probably the most significant, because money symbolizes all that's traditionally been wrong with being a secretary. It's a reflection of being overlooked and undervalued. But, while money is a big issue, it's not the barrier between support staff and job satisfaction.

We are really talking about the whole issue of support staff motivation. Of course, a motivated secretary or assistant is the only key to a successful, productive support staff/manager relationship. So far, you already will have picked up many cues as to how to motivate support staff. Maintaining an overall perspective of support professionals as valuable, contributing members of your work team goes a long way toward ensuring continuing contentment. To recap, here are actions we've already discussed that display your commitment to a modern view:

Fully utilize your secretary's skills, talents and abilities:
- Recognize the difference between technical, administrative and discretionary skills.
- Identify your assistant's particular abilities and special talents.
- Delegate work that takes advantage of your assistant's capabilities.

Encourage your secretary's creativity and professional growth:
- Seek your secretary's ideas, suggestions and opinions.
- Provide opportunities for training.
- Allow your secretary to practice newly learned skills.

Communicate:
- Tell your secretary or assistant what he or she needs to know.
- Provide meaningful feedback.
- Keep the lines of communication open.

As for the big picture, two surveys are instructive on the question of support staff and satisfaction. Professional Training Associates, publisher of *The Office Professional,* asked 661 secretaries at the 1989 convention of Professional Secretaries International to rate the importance of 12 benefits intended to enhance work performance. Monetary benefits were far from top choices: profit-sharing ranked fifth, cash bonuses eighth, and a 15% pay increase was ranked tenth in importance. Of most importance were support for professional organizations (ranking first) and ongoing training—training not just for themselves (ranked second), but for their managers (ranked third).

A Gallup survey of current, former and potential members of Professional Secretaries International completed the previous year found that more respondents in every segment named "pay" as the greatest issue facing office professionals today—more than any other issue. When asked to choose the one most important issue among three selected issues—equitable pay, recognition or the need for career paths—two out of five current members chose recognition, while about the same proportion of former and potential members chose career paths first. An average of 64% of respondent groups felt that company recognition had increased in the past five years, and the largest number of respondents in every category said that recognition had come through higher salaries. Promotions and new titles were also mentioned as means of recognition.

Later in this chapter we will discuss what's going on in progressive companies concerning support staff career ladders and titles. Chapter 7 will discuss how training and development can help meet the career advancement needs of support staff while also benefiting your company. For now, let's tackle the big issue: support staff compensation.

Compensation—the Number One Issue

Support staff and salaries—an area where it's going to take a lot to set things straight. Support staff have some legitimate complaints in this area, and compensation issues are complex. Here is some background.

Despite the growing shortage of qualified candidates, the law of supply and demand has not significantly increased support staff salary levels for a variety of reasons. According to E. James Brennan, a pay-practice consultant and recognized expert on secretarial compensation with Brennan, Thomsen Associates, of St. Louis, Missouri, one difficulty is the lack of a consistent definition of the secretary's duties. Another is the desperate or marginal candidate who accepts a lower-than-appropriate salary just to get a foot in the door. Then there's the organization that lowers its standards, thereby justifying low salary levels, rather than spending the time and money to attract and retain hard-to-find qualified secretaries. The bottom line is that supply and demand establish a minimum threshold for secretarial pay below which you can't hire anyone. Above the threshold, Brennan says, "it's complete anarchy."

What rules secretarial salaries above market minimum level, according to Brennan, are an organization's internal priorities governing the secretarial skills it values and how managers are encouraged to utilize their support staff. Brennan believes that 80% of secretarial compensation issues could be resolved if companies were consistent about the parameters of support staff jobs. An office support professional would add that if an agreed-upon standard doesn't reflect an enlightened view, it still would be unfair and inaccurate, even if it *were* consistent.

Another issue is that secretarial salaries remain low because the profession is female-dominated. Brennan confirms that social custom and economic history prove that a job performed by a woman is still perceived as less valuable than a similar job done by a man.

Accepted pay practice dictates that salaries should be tied to the officially designated duties of a position and to their performance, yet many companies still determine support staff salaries according to the level of the manager reported to—the so-called "rug ranking" system. However, according to N. E. Fried and Associates, Inc., a compensation consulting firm in Dublin, Ohio, companies are finally moving away from this unfair system.

A 1990 study of 582 compensation planners conducted by the Fried firm found that 32% of responding companies, as compared with 47% in 1988, still pay secretaries according to the organizational level of their manager. The 1990 study further reports that 37% use straight job content as a basis for compensation as compared with 29% in 1988. Twenty-nine percent of those in the 1990 study use a hybrid system, a combination of job content for lower-level support positions and rug ranking for those reporting to senior management, compared with 15% in 1988. The remaining small percentages in both studies use either market pricing or secretary's length of service.

Fried believes that companies who stick to the report-to system despite the quickly changing role of support staff are, in her words, "sitting on a potential time bomb." Fried writes:

> Because of built-in inequities, the level-of-management approach to secretarial grading perpetuates restricted pay levels and limits career opportunities. Such conditions not only make companies vulnerable to unionization and discrimination claims, but they also have caused a decline in office education enrollments and encourage many secretaries to flee the field.*

---

*"Determining Secretarial Pay," by N. Elizabeth Fried, Ph.D. *The Secretary*, August/September 1988, pp. 12–13. See Appendix for information on ordering the full report, entitled "Secretarial Pay Practices: 1990 Update."

Improvements in support staff pay scales and practices take time. There are, however, ways you can help ensure that money issues will not come between you and your secretary or assistant even if your company is behind the times.

Your first concern (if you have control or at least influence over setting salary) is that the salary you offer is competitive within your geographic area, industry and type of company. It's difficult to provide specific guidelines for support staff salaries because of significant geographic differences and the fact that any figures quoted could change so rapidly.

As a guide, see the tables on page 125 indicating the results of the 1990 nationwide Help Wanted Survey conducted for Professional Secretaries International by Dartnell Corporation's Institute of Business Research and *From Nine to Five*.

Generally, the larger the employer in terms of sales revenues and profits and the larger the metropolitan area, the higher the pay. Certain industries traditionally pay support staff at different levels: for example, advertising, retailing, banking, entertainment, fashion, cosmetic and other glamour fields tend to pay lower salaries; transportation, utilities, manufacturing, financial, legal and consulting firms pay on the higher end of the spectrum. The higher the inherent reward or prestige of working in the industry, the lower the pay.

To compare the salary you offer with the general marketplace, start with the help-wanted section of your local newspaper. Area wage surveys are often available, and a local chapter of Professional Secretaries International (see Appendix) may provide competitive data. A reliable recruiter also can provide guidance on what constitutes a competitive salary in your situation.

A big part of determining salary requires you to understand the value of the particular job. Brennan recommends that a manager who cares to ensure that a support professional is being appropriately compensated should determine how much would be paid to a man with the same credentials and doing the same type of work (excluding transcription) in terms of span of control, the ability to operate independently, set schedules, monitor and control the executive's time, and to act as proxy in the executive's absence.

Ask the questions: "What is the value added to the executive's effectiveness by the secretary? How much is it worth to the organization?" If the answer is a salary that is considered too high for a highly qualified secretary, then ask: "Can the organization afford a secretary who requires such close supervision or has such limited abilities that it's going to take even more of the executive's time rather than help better utilize it?" Or "Isn't it worth an appropriate salary to hire someone qualified to free up the executive to better accomplish his or her goals?"

Finally, you must deal with how your own value system meshes with that of your company. A problem can arise where you hire a highly qualified support professional and find that you are restricted from paying an appropriate salary because you are using the person beyond the company's expected standard. This, of course, can translate into a secretary or assistant who is thrilled with the work but becomes unhappy, frustrated and ultimately bitter and angry about the salary.

It's important that you know what your company endorses as the standard duties of a support position, to understand its limits and to know how much a secretary can do above and beyond those limits for it to be considered the same job. Making this clear right off the bat can head off later trouble resulting from an imbalance of expectations.

Support professionals want a competitive salary that accurately reflects the value of their capabilities, experience, responsibilities and job performance. Do your best to provide just that. If your hands are tied because of situations beyond your control, there are ways to work around the problem. Read on for ideas that can help you beat the money issue.

A Broad View of Compensation—Perks and Privileges

Support staff are motivated to work hard for managers who care that they are appropriately compensated. Take an active part in determining how your company will remunerate your secretary or assistant in terms of salary and other benefits. Do your best to ensure your secretary or assistant receives the maximum you believe he or she is entitled to, according to his or her value to you.

Negotiate on your secretary's behalf for raises or other benefits (examples of which follow) and fight for what you consider appropriate—don't just make casual recommendations. Even if you don't always succeed, your effort shows that support staff satisfaction matters to you and will go a long way in building goodwill.

If, as already discussed, you are kept from providing what you consider an appropriate salary, try to win other benefits from the company to make up the difference. If your company fails to come through, think about judiciously providing benefits out of your own pocket. Consider it an investment in your career and find creative ways to make up for a less-than-satisfactory salary.

If it is appropriate in your company setting, you can simply supplement a salary in cash. Periodic cash bonuses can be even more effective if timed carefully, such as at times other than holidays, in recognition of work anniversaries, or upon completion of a particularly difficult assignment.

Bonuses don't have to be in cash; your situation may be better suited to other kinds of supplements. A secretary may have an eye on something you can pay for. Take the case of Karen. Karen and her boss, Ann, had just finished putting together a large client presentation that required working late for more than a week. When the project was completed, Ann told Karen she wanted to do something to show her appreciation, but didn't know what would please Karen most. A leather briefcase had caught Karen's eye earlier that week and she mentioned it to Ann. Ann said, "Go pick it up for yourself on me."

Perhaps you have access to perks through your work or personal life you can extend to your secretary. One attorney who represents the owner of a major theater chain shares with his secretary access to prime theater tickets that are available on a moment's notice through the client. Another manager, whose husband worked in the travel business, was able to extend travel discounts to her secretary. If you think about it, you're sure to come up with something of value to which you have easy access that can be extended to your secretary or assistant.

One valuable perk that not only benefits support staff, but you and your company as well, is payment of membership dues to a professional association, such as Professional Secretaries International (PSI). Many people complain they want to take part in professional organizations and related events but can't afford to. Professional associations provide many avenues for supplementing a salary. In addition to covering membership dues, you or your company can pay for your assistant's monthly dinner meetings, registration and travel expenses to conferences and conventions, and fees for seminars and other events sponsored by the association.

Sponsorship in an organization that serves to further professional growth and development provides you with a valuable payback and also conveys a belief in support staff professionalism, which is one of your primary goals as a modern boss. Point out to management the value of sponsoring membership for all support staff in the firm—this is a prime benefit worth fighting for.

If your secretary or assistant isn't ready to make a commitment to an organization, you could pay for a subscription to a professional journal, such as *The Secretary*®*, or one of the many other newsletters published for secretaries (see Appendix). Your secretary probably receives frequent mailings about such newsletters and other programs and services directed to secretaries, if you need other ideas.

Another valued perk rarely offered to support staff is compensatory time off. If your secretary or assistant has been working above and beyond the call of duty, offer a long weekend, an afternoon off or an extended lunch hour and don't charge the time to official vacation or personal time. Use your discretionary power. Allow flexibility in working hours when possible. An extra hour in the morning or an occasional short afternoon is very much appreciated by support staff who usually work by the clock, unlike most other people in the office. Compensatory time off is especially appreciated when a person doesn't have to ask for it. Take the initiative and offer—it's a more effective motivator that way.

Giving Recognition and Showing Appreciation

Recognition and appreciation are very important to support staff. As mentioned earlier, examples of higher forms of recognition include higher salaries, promotions and new titles. A manager should also think about giving recognition on a small scale, however. Giving recognition doesn't have to mean banquets, speeches and honors bestowed. In fact, going overboard with good intentions can backfire because support professionals react negatively to patronizing. Recognition should occur on a regular basis and not wait until a once-a-year review or the Professional Secretaries Day. One secretary, Carolyn, describes why she was so satisfied working with one former boss:

> He was generous with praise, always gave recognition and credit to those who earned it, and always backed up his praise with monetary compensation and/or promotions when the

---

*A trademark of Professional Secretaries International.

time came. Hal always introduced me to his business associates and colleagues and gave me recognition in front of them for work I had prepared for their meetings. In return, he almost never had to ask me to stay late or come in on a weekend. When it was apparent to me that he needed me, I would approach him to ask whether he needed me to stay. I was rarely ill during the years I worked with him, and I think a lot of this has to do with contentment.

Seemingly small gestures, such as being introduced to clients and associates, as Carolyn mentioned, help fulfill a support professional's need for recognition. Being personally informed of the outcome of projects is also important. If your secretary or assistant has worked with you on a long, difficult project, don't let him or her hear of its consequence third-hand or by accident—give the news yourself. And make sure you include support staff in a project's wrap-up meetings or celebrations, whether they be preplanned parties or spur-of-the-moment gatherings in your office. Of course, always remember to give credit where credit is due. Recognize support staff contributions to a project in front of people who count.

You need to show appreciation of all your secretary or assistant does for you, especially for special favors not considered and agreed on in advance as part of the job, such as running personal errands, volunteering to work through lunch, coming in early or staying late.

When it comes to recognition and appreciation, good intentions can easily and often do go awry. You can get into trouble by forgetting that you are a modern manager and reverting to inappropriate thank-yous better saved for personal relationships: sending a card, buying flowers or candy, or taking your secretary out to lunch. While these are kind gestures, some support professionals feel they aren't in line with the professional recognition they seek.

Appreciation means more than just saying "Thank you." Refer back to the guidelines for providing meaningful feedback discussed in Chapter 4, and also to the section in this chapter on perks for support staff, for appropriate ways to show your appreciation. Above all, don't wait until Professional Secretaries Day to recognize your secretary or assistant. If you use and abuse your secretary all year and think you can make things right on this one day, you're bound for trouble.

Don't Forget Professional Secretaries Week

The dilemma of how to appropriately show appreciation becomes particularly acute during Professional Secretaries Week. It's hard to know what to do, especially when you are bombarded with advertisements emphasizing the card-and-flowers approach. It's true, support staff are often happy with this sort of gesture. Sometimes any attention at all is welcome because support staff so often feel overlooked. Again, flowers are nice, but it's not enough to show you believe in what this week is intended for.

It's good for you to understand what Professional Secretaries Day®* and Professional Secretaries Week®* are really all about. National Secretaries Week, as it was originally called, was initiated in 1952 by the president of the National Secretaries Association (now known as PSI) and the president of Dictaphone Corporation, who were working on a council to address the national shortage of skilled office workers.

The two approached the U.S. Secretary of Commerce, Charles Sawyer, about proclaiming a National Secretaries Week with the purpose of recognizing ". . . the American secretary, upon whose skills, loyalty and efficiency the functions of business and government depend." The objective, to call attention, "through favorable publicity, to the tremendous potential of the secretarial career."

Support professionals are pleased to see, however, that in recent years attention to the day has taken on a more contemporary tenor, focusing on the challenges faced by support staff and the organizations they serve in the information age and the automated office.

To the true support professional, the purpose of Professional Secretaries Week is to draw attention to the fact that it's time to take a contemporary perspective of support staff and to give up, once and for all, the secretarial stereotype. The hope among many is that in the not-too-distant future, Professional Secretaries Week will no longer be needed, because there will no longer be a stereotype to fight.

What is an appropriate way to mark these events? Your best bet is to watch for what's going on in your area that reflects the intended spirit of the day and week.

*Professional Secretaries Day and Professional Secretaries Week are trademarks of Professional Secretaries International.

Local Chambers of Commerce often sponsor some type of luncheon awards event in which area companies are invited to participate. A recent trend has been the combination benefit/recognition lunch or dinner, such as the "All Star Salute to Secretaries" put on jointly by chapters of the Arthritis Foundation and Professional Secretaries International.

Many seminars also are offered during the week. One example is the American Management Association's "Seminar by Satellite" videoconference, in which secretaries in cities across the country simultaneously participate in a program in honor of the day. If you pay attention to the mail that crosses your desk during the few weeks prior to Professional Secretaries Week, you will certainly get some good ideas.

Even if you are unable to attend such an event with your secretary or assistant, you can still send him or her to a seminar or other event. A good example is a biannual event sponsored by Professional Secretaries International called "Secretary Speakout." At Speakout events, support staff from all over the country gather to discuss and reach a consensus statement on a topic relevant to the profession. You can obtain information on Speakout and other events being sponsored by PSI in your area by calling PSI headquarters in Kansas City at (816) 891-6600.

Even if your company routinely recognizes support staff in honor of the week, you must still do something for your own assistant. This is especially true when the company chooses a less-than-professional approach (as is often the case) and gives each secretary a plant or something else not entirely appropriate.

The personnel director of one large law firm was pleased to have approval from management to spend much more money than the usual budgeted amount (as a result of intensive persuasion and persistence) for tokens of appreciation in honor of Professional Secretaries Week. Expensive candy was purchased (not a recommended choice and not much of an improvement over the usual plant). To each package was attached a personally typed note of appreciation from "management."

While some secretaries believed the choice of candy was inappropriate, overall reception of the gesture was very positive. Why? Not because of the candy, but because of the personally typed and signed notes. *That* was what mattered most—that someone cared enough to type and sign a note of appreciation just for each person.

124 • WORK WITH ME!

From a professional's point of view, attending a seminar or other appropriate event is highly preferable to gifts, but if gift-buying is the norm in your company, it's all right to go along so long as the gift reflects professionalism. Here are some gift suggestions for a wide range of budgets (some of which were mentioned when we discussed perks):

- Subscription to a professional journal or serious magazine; i.e., *The Secretary*.
- Quality pen and pencil set.
- Desk outfit—blotter, pen holder, etc.
- Leather organizer or calendar.
- Attaché case or leather tote bag.
- Reimbursement of fees for a course or seminar that will further your secretary's professional growth.
- Membership dues in a professional association.
- Reimbursement of expenses for a conference, convention, exhibition or other event relevant to your industry or the secretarial profession.

Mark Professional Secretaries Week (the last full week in April) and Professional Secretaries Day (Wednesday of that week) on your calendar. No matter how you choose to honor your secretary or assistant, don't let those important dates pass unnoticed!

GOOD MANAGER BEHAVIORS

Here are more guidelines for building a successful relationship with your secretary.

Between You and Your Secretary

Explaining Decisions. Whenever possible, provide background to decisions you've made so support staff can better understand and identify with them. If you decide that your secretary or assistant can't take off a certain week for vacation, for example, explain your reasoning. Simply laying down the law only makes a person feel like a child with you as parent—precisely opposite from the team experience you're trying to create.

ANNUAL SALARY RANGES BY TITLE
(rounded to the nearest dollar)

Title	Quoted Salary Range	Average Salary Range
Administrative assistant	$10,400–$40,000	$23,402–$24,450
Executive secretary	$14,000–$45,000	$26,894–$27,654
Administrative secretary	$15,000–$45,000	$25,199–$28,466
Secretary/receptionist	$12,480–$28,800	$18,091–$20,654
Secretary	$10,000–$70,000	$20,593–$24,927

ANNUAL SALARY RANGES BY CITY
(rounded to the nearest dollar)

City	Quoted Salary Range	Average Salary Range
Chicago, IL	$12,480–$40,000	$23,180–$26,289
New York, NY	$13,000–$70,000	$28,183–$30,237
St. Louis, MO	$10,000–$50,000	$16,500–$20,143
Miami, FL	$12,480–$32,000	$21,570–$24,737
Dallas, TX	$12,480–$32,000	$19,629–$23,133
Cleveland, OH	$10,400–$26,000	$17,148–$20,628
Atlanta, GA	$12,500–$40,000	$19,817–$24,716
Philadelphia, PA	$14,017–$35,000	$21,036–$24,322
Memphis, TN	$12,000–$23,000	$15,326–$15,928
Denver, CO	$12,240–$32,000	$16,926–$19,974
Des Moines, IA	$12,480–$32,000	$17,609–$23,700
Kansas City, MO	$10,400–$26,000	$17,124–$18,760
Los Angeles, CA	$14,000–$37,000	$24,167–$27,540
Seattle, WA	$12,480–$30,000	$20,134–$20,386
Toronto, ON	$22,000–$28,500	$24,000–$25,250
Montreal, PB	$15,600–$34,000	$23,288–$27,063
Vancouver, BC	$12,000–$36,000	$22,216–$23,931

NEWSPAPERS SURVEYED:
United States: *Chicago Tribune, New York Times, St. Louis Post-Dispatch, Miami Herald, Dallas Morning News, Cleveland Plain Dealer, Atlanta Journal/Constitution, Philadelphia Inquirer, Memphis Commercial Appeal, Denver Post, Des Moines Register, Kansas City Star, Los Angeles Times, Seattle Times.*
Canada: *Toronto Star, Vancouver Sun, Montreal Gazette.*
Survey results courtesy of *From Nine to Five*, The Dartnell Corporation, 4660 North Ravenswood Avenue, Chicago, Ill. 60640, (800) 621-5463.

This also applies to decisions that come down from upper management. If you're aware of the rationale behind rulings mandated from above, share the background with support staff. This will nip in the bud negativism about the decision as well as eliminate the effects of grapevine guessing as to what's going on.

To go even a step further, include support staff in decisions that involve them. It is, of course, well accepted management philosophy that participating in decision-making means better acceptance of and compliance with decisions.

Respecting Privacy. "Secretaries" and "privacy" are two words that don't go together very well. Lack of privacy is an occupational hazard for support staff because of the way most offices are set up. Notice that most support staff sit at a desk out in the open somewhere close to the manager's office. Sometimes there are makeshift cubicles or other efforts made to provide a somewhat closed environment, but rarely do support staff have their own offices.

Being left out in the open makes support staff vulnerable to continual observation by others and creates a lack of privacy that can be very disturbing. No one enjoys working with someone looking over their shoulder. If your secretary or assistant is situated just outside your door, arrange your desk so that you are not looking right out at him or her. Do whatever you can within your space limitations to provide as much privacy as possible.

One of the problems that results from being out in the open is that support staff are often almost too available. Someone who has an office has the option of closing the door. Even if the door is open, visitors are expected to knock before entering. But the secretary's desk is all too easy to approach. Support staff in these situations tend to feel exposed, vulnerable and generally uncomfortable. Many secretaries complain that even if they're on the phone, people just walk up and stand there listening to the conversation, waiting for the call to end, or, worse, interrupt the phone conversation. This is boldly rude behavior, but it happens all the time.

One secretary had a painfully amusing story to tell that illustrates how lack of privacy can turn into continual frustration. Laurie's desk is situated right out in the open. She complains that people think nothing of walking right up to her desk and interrupting her for the silliest things. One day a manager approached as Laurie was busy working on a document and interrupted her to ask her where her out box was. The out box was right behind Laurie with a 12-by-3-inch bright yellow sign with OUT BOX posted above it. To support staff, this kind of behavior reflects an attitude that says it's okay to interrupt secretaries since what they do isn't very important.

Whether your own setup is particularly good or bad, there are ways you can help the situation. For one thing, don't run out to your secretary's desk every time you think of something to say, ask or assign. If you have an intercom, use it. But use the intercom wisely. If you can see that your secretary or assistant is on the phone, allow a minute or two for the call to be ended. If time goes on and the call doesn't end, call on the intercom or slip a note asking your secretary or assistant to see you when he or she is free.

Further, respect your secretary's "space." Don't touch things on his or her desk or go through drawers or files unless you have express permission to do so. People who walk up to find someone standing at their desk feel as if their privacy has been invaded, just as the manager does who walks into his or her office to find someone sitting at the desk or looking through papers on a credenza.

Staying out of the Way. Here's another situation that is complicated by a secretary's overavailability. Once you've assigned certain projects, for heaven's sake, leave your secretary or assistant alone as much as possible to do the work. If you've clearly explained what you want done, there's no need to keep checking up. As you're giving initial instructions, be sure to tell your secretary or assistant to come to you with questions or problems. Then trust him or her to follow through. This is not to say you shouldn't be allowed to ask for progress reports. Find a comfortable medium—don't run out every 10 minutes and ask, "Is it finished yet?"

Support staff don't enjoy working with managers who are constantly underfoot. Don't continually impose your presence on your secretary. Many managers are unconsciously in the way. In one office, this was a continual problem between June, the manager, and Cathy, her secretary. The managers' mail in this office was distributed to the desk of each manager's secretary. The secretaries' desks were designed with a chest-high partition at the front with a foot-wide ledge on top—ironically, to provide the secretary with a little privacy. June had a habit of coming out to look at her mail, which was stacked on a ledge at the front of Cathy's desk.

June would open, sort and read her mail while standing at Cathy's desk, violating her privacy and causing her anxiety. As she read the mail, she'd reach onto Cathy's desk for a paper clip, a pencil, the stapler, the Rolodex for a number and even the phone to make a call. Further, June would make comments to Cathy about whatever she was reading, distracting her from the work she was trying to get done. Then she'd go into her office and ask, "Is that letter done yet?"

Clearly, June's behavior is unconscious. Make sure you're not thoughtlessly doing something that keeps support staff from accomplishing their work. In short, stay out of the way.

Giving the Benefit of the Doubt. We touched on this area in connection with trust, but it bears repeating as a good manager behavior. Remember that your secretary is on your side. If there's really a problem, talk about it. But don't jump to conclusions about support staff behavior.

If it seems your secretary or assistant is on the phone a great deal, don't automatically assume you're being taken advantage of. People often think that whenever a secretary is on the phone, the call is personal. A lot of support staff work happens to be conducted by telephone. Yes, support staff sometimes do make personal calls, but they're not alone. In any event, it doesn't necessarily mean that the privilege is being abused.

Always think before you approach. If you feel you must intervene, inquire—don't accuse. For example, say you've asked your secretary or assistant to summarize a stack of reports for your committee meeting. The meeting is to be held at 3:00 P.M.; it's now 1:00 P.M., you haven't received the summary and your secretary is standing at the desk of another secretary talking.

Number one, don't assume what they're talking about is personal. It may be, it may not. Second, don't take the attitude that regardless of what they're talking about, what you have to say is more important. Support staff often complain about being treated as lesser human beings, and this is an often-cited case in point. Give support staff the chance to prove they are capable of meeting deadlines and managing time without your intervention. What should matter is results, not methods.

Following Through on Promises. If you say you're going to do something, do it. Just because you haven't used the word "promise" doesn't mean this rule doesn't apply. Here are some common areas where support staff complain their managers have let them down:

- "We'll go through that pile of paper this week."
- "We'll talk about your vacation tomorrow."
- "I'll look into ordering you a new printer tomorrow."
- "I'll talk to the supervisor about your raise/promotion/title change next week."
- "We'll talk about your request to handle more projects soon."
- "You'll have some time off as soon as things calm down."
- "Give me a proposal on that idea and I'll consider it."
- "Put that proposal in writing and I'll take it to my supervisor."
- "We'll review your proposal to hire a part-time assistant at the beginning of next week."
- "If we get this account, I'll see that you get a bonus for your efforts."
- "This is the last time I'll interrupt you today."

Many secretaries have difficulty reminding a manager of what he or she promised to do. Just because you don't hear about it, doesn't mean your secretary or assistant has forgotten what you said. He or she may be stewing over the fact that time continues to go by without your action. Frustration can build; attitudes can sour, and the relationship can start down the tubes.

If you are unable to act within a given time frame, at least give your secretary an indication that you're aware of the situation, that you intend to follow through and that you have a plan for dealing with it.

Reciprocating Favors. The manager who takes the "we're equals" rather than a "me king, you slave" approach is best accepted by support staff. Find ways to reciprocate favors your secretary or assistant does for you. For instance, Susan regularly did Jim's banking, something that wasn't in Susan's job description and that saved Jim a lot of time. Since time was the issue, Jim thought of ways in which he could repay Susan with time—such as offering her extra time at lunch on payday in which to do her own banking.

Showing an Interest. A common complaint of support staff is being treated like nonpersons. Remember that support professionals are not just there for you to order around. Don't shut them out.

Support staff will feel left out, for instance, to hear through a third party that you closed on a new house. And a secretary will feel put out if he or she's the star on the company softball team and you never ask how the team did the night before.

It can be difficult to determine just how far one should go in showing an interest. You do need to find a business and personal balance in the relationship. On the one hand, it is important for you to show a genuine interest in your secretary's activities outside of work, but, then again, going too far in discussing personal lives could undermine the professionalism of your relationship.

You should definitely take an interest, for example, in anything your secretary or assistant does on the outside to further his or her professional growth and development, such as seminars, evening classes or association memberships. Some personal interest is appropriate too, however. Take five minutes, for example, on Monday morning to find out how the weekend was. Not that you should sit through a play-by-play of every activity, but at least get a rundown on the overall experience. This will not only show interest, but also give you a clue as to your secretary's state of mind on Monday morning. On Friday afternoon, casually ask whether anything special is planned for the weekend. Again, don't encourage too much detail; just show you realize there is life outside the office.

It is appropriate to be aware of your secretary's family situation in general, as well as any special family problems, such as illness or difficult situations with children or other family members. You should not, however, be subjected to detailed daily reports. A brief inquiry as to how well things are going is enough; stay away from getting too specific or being drawn in as a counselor or adviser. Your interest shows concern; your keeping out of it shows you respect his or her ability to handle the situation.

Show human consideration, but don't be taken advantage of. If your secretary or assistant is too willing to provide more information than you care to hear, tactfully bring the conversation around to a work-related topic. He or she will eventually pick up on your cue.

Draw the line when it comes to your respective romantic lives and discussions concerning finances. Remember, although you work closely together, you are above all else the boss, not a friend. You should be friendly, but developing a real friendship can interfere with the superior/subordinate nature of the relationship.

Successfully striking a business/personal balance in your relationship can create an effective tightness about your team. Showing an interest can not only strengthen your relationship, but serve as yet another weapon in fighting off the coffee klatch. Remember, if your secretary feels isolated, he or she will head in their direction. All it takes on your part is a few well-chosen words to show you know a secretary is a person, too.

A Secretary's Pet Peeves

This will summarize the flip side of good manager behaviors in case you need a quick reference for comparing your behavior.

Interruptions. Granted, to some degree it's the nature of the secretary's job to be at the whim of the manager; after all, support staff work in large measure depends on the momentary needs of the manager. But remember to use good judgment—restrain yourself from needlessly or inappropriately interrupting support staff as they try to complete work assignments.

Procrastination. We have said that it is all right to be a procrastinator so long as you admit it. That doesn't mean support staff like procrastination—in fact, they really hate it. If you are a procrastinator, at least force yourself to tell your secretary or assistant what work assignments you should be tackling and their respective deadlines so he or she can keep after you to get on it. And there is a way to be considerate about procrastination. Support staff appreciate being warned well in advance if a serious work crunch is approaching so they may prepare for it, both mentally and in terms of juggling other work assignments.

Disorganization. In general, secretaries are by nature organized people who dislike disorganization. But it's okay if you're disorganized, because part of a support professional's job is to organize you. The key is to allow your secretary or assistant to do just that. Religiously conform with whatever systems and controls your secretary institutes to keep you organized. And apologize profusely when you're occasionally out of organizational control.

Inconsistency. Do what you say you're going to do. And be predictable in work-related matters. A secretary needs to know how a manager will react in order to anticipate needs and act in the manager's absence.

Disloyalty. Stand up for support staff when the need arises. Good managers never say anything about support staff in their absence that they wouldn't say in their presence.

Isolation. Don't overlook, ignore or shut out your secretary.

Condescension. There's no excuse for this one.

Being Taken for Granted. Never take your secretary or anyone else for granted. Recognize and appreciate your secretary every day, not just on Professional Secretaries Day.

THE OFFICE PICTURE

What is it like for a secretary to work for your company? Chapter 1 discussed common organizational practices that are less than desirable from a support staff point of view. More than likely, your company is guilty of at least a few of the infractions mentioned. Since you want a satisfied and motivated assistant, it's in your best interest to ensure that your secretary or assistant is protected from organizational mishandling.

Support staff today are encouraged to be assertive in going after what they want from a company, yet experience shows that they usually get nowhere without a manager's support, especially in a company that still seems to be in the Dark Ages. It's up to you to use your influence, make up for shortcomings and get around roadblocks in the system for your secretary's benefit.

To recap, the main areas where companies often fall short include:

- Appropriate compensation.
- Properly distinguishing secretarial positions.
- Recognizing individual contributions of secretaries.
- Offering opportunity for career advancement.
- Drawing support staff in as a true part of the organization.

Here is information about what some companies are doing to remedy problem areas and some suggestions for bridging the gap between what your company offers and what support staff want and need.

Support Staff Levels and Titles

An overly vague title or classification that doesn't accurately reflect the nature of a support professional's job may become a problem, especially when the secretary has reached the salary ceiling of the classification.

The 1990 N. E. Fried study found that it was most common to find between three and five secretarial levels within companies, with a little over 67% of responding companies falling into the three- to five-level category. The largest number of companies, representing 26.1%, had four secretarial levels. The highest number of levels reported was 13, in only one responding company. It was also noted that companies using secretarial levels to distinguish among positions also tended to use the job content system of determining secretarial salary. While 38% of responding companies in the Fried study had some exempt secretaries, most companies had only one exempt level. See the Appendix for further information on this report, which includes descriptions for secretarial job families and title options.

In the fall of 1988, Professional Secretaries International conducted an exercise entitled "What's in a Name?" at its district level conferences. The result was a comprehensive list of possible titles held by support staff professionals around the country, grouped according to career path specialty.

Entry Level

Bookkeeper
Clerk/typist
Data entry clerk
File clerk
Junior clerk
Junior secretary
Keypunch operator
Mail clerk
Purchasing clerk

Receptionist/secretary
Secretary
Senior clerk
Stenographer
Switchboard operator
Transcriptionist
 (medical/legal)
Typist
Word processing pool

Administrative

Accounting clerk
Administrative aide
Administrative analyst
Administrative assistant
Administrative manager
Administrative officer
Administrative professional
Administrative secretary
Administrative services officer/manager
Administrative specialist

Administrative support assistant
Administrative technician
Assistant to . . .
Benefits administrator/coordinator
Chief executive secretary
Communications coordinator
Conference planner/coordinator
Confidential assistant
Corporate secretary
Corresponding secretary

134 • WORK WITH ME!

Department secretary
Executive administrator
Executive assistant
Executive secretary
Executive support secretary
Executive support specialist
Internal public relations manager
Inventory record-keeper
Junior office administrator
Logistics coordinator
Management support specialist
Marketing assistant
Meeting planner
Office administrator
Office assistant
Office coordinator
Office manager

Payroll clerk
Personnel analyst
Personnel officer
Personnel records administrator
Personnel specialist
Project administrator
Project coordinator
Records manager
Sales assistant
Secretary to . . .
Senior administrator
Senior office administrator
Senior secretary
Staff assistant
Staff relations analyst
Travel coordinator

Technical

Computer operator
Computer technician
Copy center operator
Database administrator
Data conversion processor
Data conversion technician
Data processing clerk
Desktop publisher
Document coordinator
Document processing manager
Document production specialist
Graphics specialist
Information manager
Information processing specialist
Information systems analyst
Information systems assistant
Key punch operator
Lead operator

Legal secretary
Loan secretary
Medical secretary
Office automation coordinator
Office systems specialist/technologist
Office technician
Quality control assistant
Research specialist
Senior technical clerk
Staff accountant
Systems administrator
Systems programmer
Systems technologist
Technical adviser
Technical writer
Word processing specialist
Word processor

Training

Business educator
Career counselor
Clerical consultant
Continuing education
    administrator/coordinator
Department training specialist
Educational coordinator
Education specialist

Employee development specialist
Human resource officer
In-house educator
Management support specialist
Office automation trainer
Office environment specialist
Office support trainer
Orientation administrator

Personnel assistant
Personnel officer
Procedures training specialist
Professional development specialist
Quality control specialist
Recruitment specialist
Secretarial trainer I, II
Seminar coordinator
Staff development instructor
Staff development officer

Staff training assistant
Staff training coordinator
Training assistant
Training coordinator
Training facilitator
Training instructor
Training officer
Training specialist
Training systems specialist
Word processing trainer

Support staff need not only your support to fight for a reclassification or change in title, but hard evidence as well. The solution goes back to a large part of the problem: most companies do not have accurate job descriptions for secretaries, if they have them at all. Have your secretary or assistant create a job description for the position.

Creating a Job Description

Valid job descriptions result from in-depth job analysis, not from merely sitting down and writing a list of duties from memory. Three steps must be followed: data collection, analysis and summary. You can't get to Step Three without first following through on Steps One and Two, especially when it comes to support staff work (remember the influence of the stereotype and the perception gap).

If you're starting completely from scratch with no job description, valid or not, you might want to refer to the prototype secretarial job description that has been prepared by Professional Secretaries International (see Appendix). The prototype can be modified to suit your specific situation, using the same process outlined below.

STEP ONE: Data Collection. Have your secretary keep a detailed log of daily activities. Entries should be made into this "Daily Journal" (see Appendix) faithfully for a minimum of one month, preferably two. The object is to record every move that's made in the course of a day. Here are the rules:

1. Record *everything*—including the most trivial activities.
2. *Be specific*—i.e., don't just write down "Answered the

phone," but include who called and the outcome of the conversation.
3. Pay close attention to communications of all kinds, oral and written, again including names.
4. IMPORTANT: Make entries as you work. Don't wait until later—you won't remember what you did.

Your assistant should be instructed not to read over the journal until at least a month, preferably two, has passed. Reading a few days' or even two weeks' worth of notes won't tell much. But over a good length of time, definite patterns will emerge.

STEP TWO: Analysis. The next step is to review carefully the journals and categorize activities. If possible, it's helpful if you and your secretary or assistant do this step together. It's also helpful to read completely through the journal pages a couple of times in order to process the information before attempting the actual categorizing. The categories themselves should make themselves evident. Here are some examples to help get started:

- Office administration
- Client development
- Client relations
- Document drafting, editing, proofreading or abstracting
- Financial
- Information management
- Meeting arrangement or preparation
- Project work
- Research
- Travel arrangement or preparation

Start with a readily apparent category and search for all journal entries that apply. Work with one or two categories at a time, rather than going through line by line and attempting to assign each to a category. As an entry is assigned to a category, check it off.

STEP 3: Summary. Once the material is categorized, the final step is to put the information into a logical order. Group related categories together and list duties and responsibilities in order of priority, or whatever you deem appropriate. Additional sections may be added giving an overall job summary—how the position fits into the department, to whom the secretary reports and others who are supported in addition to the principal—and the equipment utilized by the secretary. Your assistant's job description is finished.

You may wonder whether all this effort is worth the risk of opening this can of worms. It is possible, of course, that management will pay no attention whatsoever to your new job description. Make it clear to your secretary from the start that the job description won't guarantee the desired results. It will, in any event, offer many other benefits to secretaries and managers.

First, support staff very often gain a new respect for their own job, since they have, maybe for the first time, a true understanding of how their work impacts on the manager's, department's and company's goals. And an accurate job description can serve as a springboard for most effective use of support staff and development of untapped potential. Coordinating effort and expanding responsibilities take on new meaning when you have a solid base from which to start.

The job description can also prove invaluable in the performance appraisal process, the next area in which you can positively influence the support staff experience within your company.

The Performance Appraisal

Support staff, like all other employees, anticipate that evaluation time of year. Not only because appraisal time is often also raise time, although that certainly is a factor, but because they look forward to a meaningful discussion with their managers about how they're doing and what's in the cards for them in the coming year. Don't let your secretary or assistant down in this important area. If your company's evaluation practices are unsatisfactory to support staff, their frustration and poor attitude will focus on you. Here is some insight into what often goes wrong and guidelines for ensuring your secretary's appraisal experience is a fair and positive one.

The object in employee evaluation is to measure performance against expected standards. The first obvious problem in appraising secretarial performance is that, as discussed above, there usually is not an accurate job description against which to compare a secretary. Another problem is that a large part of what a secretary does is not easily measurable. It's therefore hard to be objective, as is the goal of modern evaluation techniques.

1. Make sure the evaluation isn't overly general. An appraisal can't be effective if it doesn't even cover what is actually done on the job. A fair evaluation must look into the specific duties of the individual's job. The evaluation shouldn't focus only on the technical aspects of the job, just because they are more readily apparent, i.e., typing and dictation speed and accuracy, etc.—discretionary skills must be included in evaluation. A few factors support staff consider particularly important: personal contact, problem-solving abilities, organizational skills, confidentiality, reliability, attitude, commitment to the organization and its goals.

2. Try to measure your secretary's contribution to the department in a meaningful way. Be objective about the subjective. Use the "critical incident method" to capture the input and effectiveness of discretionary skills—keep track, or have your secretary keep track, of actions that had particularly positive or negative consequences over the course of the appraisal period.

    Here's an example that illustrates the importance of these two items. A poor evaluation form will ask for a response concerning promptness and courtesy in answering the telephone. This broad question totally overlooks the fact that the secretary in question screens incoming calls from prospective clients. He or she must use judgment in extracting information and deciding who can best help the caller. The secretary must also answer questions the caller may have, in effect serving in a sales and public relations capacity on behalf of the firm.

    By asking such a basic question, the evaluation form does not take into account the volume of calls handled nor the outcome of those calls: how many clients added or lost by the company could in fact be partially attributed to the support person. Performance in just this one area has an impact on the bottom line of the company. Evaluating that performance should somehow reflect the support professional's effectiveness in this respect.

3. Evaluation should focus on results, not methods. Criteria for evaluating support staff often are irrelevant and even offensive to them. A typical example is the question: "Is the secretary away from the work area longer than neces-

sary?" Questions like these make a secretary feel like an assembly-line worker rather than a professional. How many pressure deadlines a secretary was able to meet versus how many were missed is far more indicative of performance than how many minutes he or she was away from the desk. What should matter is what is produced, not how it is produced—allowances should be made for variations in work style.

4. Undue weight should not be given to punctuality and absenteeism. One secretary complained that in her last performance review, all but 10 minutes of a one-hour interview were spent discussing the fact that she was often 5 or 10 minutes late in the morning. No mention was made, however, of the fact that she often worked through lunch of her own accord or stayed 15 or 20 minutes late in the evening to tie up loose ends. This is an example of why support staff don't feel like team members.

   Many support staff are unaware of federal laws that may dictate company policy concerning hours of work and overtime. If this is the case, and federal restrictions are being appropriately applied, perhaps secretarial education in this area is necessary. In the absence of such restrictions, it may be helpful for the secretary to keep track of merit points for good behaviors that can counterbalance demerits received for being late or absent. In any event, these details should not take precedence over overall contribution.

5. Involve the support professional in the appraisal process. Suggest that your secretary or assistant keep his or her own evaluation documentation—a sort of daily journal already discussed. This makes the manager's job easier and helps ensure support staff have a realistic perception of their performance. You can also have your secretary fill out a self-evaluation form based on the appraisal form you use. You can then compare responses and clear up any misperceptions that may exist.

6. Performance appraisal should not just evaluate past performance, but provide guidance for improvement in the future. You know all about MBO—management by objectives. This management technique should not be reserved exclusively for management personnel. Use it with support staff. Work together to set performance goals and plans for

your assistant's growth and development. Think of your role in the process as coach, not judge.
7. The results of a performance appraisal should be shared with a secretary by the manager. In order for the review to be meaningful, the secretary should be allowed the opportunity for mutual discussion of the appraisal. Don't leave the interview to Personnel—bringing in a third party puts a wedge between support professional and manager that undermines the team spirit of the relationship. Schedule a specific time for the interview and ensure it will be uninterrupted—accord your secretary or assistant the same courtesy you would a client or colleague.

Counteracting Other Organizational Problems

If your company tends to overlook support staff, help your secretary or assistant gain positive visibility with upper management. Bring his or her accomplishments to the attention of key people within the company. Bringing talent to light can only reflect well on you. Make sure upper managers are aware of your secretary's professional development efforts. See that they know about degree work, accumulation of continuing education credits (CEU's) or the attainment of the Certified Professional Secretary (CPS) rating.

If you come up against a stereotypical attitude about support staff that seems unwavering, take the approach that your secretary is different. For example, if you seek a promotion for your secretary and meet with resistance because "secretaries are not promotable," insist that your secretary is an exception.

If your company does not get involved in career planning for secretarial staff, do the counseling yourself. Using tools already mentioned, such as a job description and the performance appraisal, help your secretary or assistant develop a long-range career plan. You may worry you'll lose a good assistant down the road, but it doesn't mean it will happen overnight. Your efforts will go far in motivating your secretary to be of the utmost value to you in the meantime. Who knows? You may be able to promote the person within your own department and not lose him or her after all.

If general company practices tend to isolate support staff, question whether such practices are written in stone. Just because support staff are not usually invited to gatherings or included in meetings does not mean they are forbidden to attend. Take the initiative and bring your secretary or assistant along.

Your efforts to keep your secretary happy in a less-than-perfect business world cast you in the roles of mentor, coach, career counselor and benefactor. These roles require little more from you than serving as catalyst and guide in your secretary's efforts toward career satisfaction. Each role adds a dimension to the support staff/manager relationship that effectively develops the kind of loyalty that results in your reaping as much, if not more, advantage as your secretary.

6 SUPPORT STAFF AND THE WOMAN MANAGER

As if the support staff/manager relationship in its evolutionary state weren't complicated enough, there's even more for the woman manager to think about. But—Attention male readers: don't think this chapter doesn't apply to you. Chances are you are or will be directly or indirectly involved with a female manager/secretary or assistant relationship. Whether you supervise women managers or share a support staff with one, you need to understand the dynamics of this special relationship.

It's a relatively simple matter to analyze the traditional male manager/secretary relationship because of its long history. But when it comes to the female boss, it's more difficult to make generalizations—it just hasn't been long enough for clear patterns to develop. At this point, support staff's perceptions about working for a woman tend to reflect individual experience rather than broadly illuminate how the relationship is different. It is possible, however, to point out potential problem areas from the woman manager's point of view.

Women are not having an easy time moving into management ranks of a male-dominated business world; secretaries are struggling to overcome, once and for all, a stereotype that has too long excluded them from their rightful place on the organizational team. The underlying issues of both campaigns collide when it comes to building and maintaining a successful secretary/manager team.

IT'S BEEN A LONG, HARD ROAD . . .

The woman manager has worked hard to earn a place on the management team, indeed, many feel, even harder than her male counterparts. To some, this meant working longer hours, giving up more lunches and working more weekends. Others have found it's not enough just to work harder; succeeding in a male-dominated management world often requires a woman to act like a man in order to fit in. For most women managers, personal sacrifices run high, but so do the rewards of success. A woman manager often feels, and rightly so, that she has "arrived," perhaps against all odds.

A manager's own experience will direct her behavior, consciously and unconsciously. The woman manager must be aware of how her actions may be received in order to avoid difficulty. Let's look at the woman manager from a secretary's point of view.

Who's Better Than Whom?

It's often said that while aggressiveness is considered a positive trait in men, the same behavior in women is perceived negatively. Support staff do complain that some women managers seem to try harder to prove themselves and are perceived as "pushy" as a result. This may simply come from preconceived notions concerning men and women on the secretary's part, perhaps combined with woman-to-woman rivalry. But it may also be a manager's unconscious arrogance. Assistants and secretaries react negatively to women bosses who have a "superior attitude"—as though they're "better" because they have "risen above" secretarial work.

What causes a manager to be judged this way? Perhaps she's overly sympathetic, devaluing the work itself; she apologizes too much for assigning what may be considered drudgery—copying, for example. Or perhaps she tends to go overboard in distancing herself from secretaries, as if being connected to them were detrimental to one's health. You must maintain a careful balance in the relationship—being overly aloof is as bad as being too friendly.

Why Isn't She Like Me?

Often the same manager who is seen as "pushy" runs into trouble because she expects the same level of commitment in her secretary that she herself has exhibited in moving up the career ladder. Some women managers, especially those who were once secretaries themselves, take it for granted that secretaries are anxious to move out of the profession, always saying things like "You're so smart—you can do better than this." One manager wrote to *Working Woman*: "My secretary is a loyal, dedicated employee. I would love to groom her for a management position. Unfortunately, she is not interested in advancing to a decision-making role. She is proud to be an executive secretary—frustrating for a feminist boss!"

A manager who openly expresses an attitude that feminism requires all women to share the same career goals can negatively reinforce a secretary's nagging worry that "it's not okay" to be a secretary. One side benefit of secretarial work, and for some a major impetus in making the profession a lifelong career, is that a secretary can be very close to the action without the weight of the responsibility that managers must bear. It just suits some people, whether because of personality, lifestyle or otherwise, not to work at a job that goes home with one every night, if one indeed goes home.

You can't necessarily expect your secretary to share your drive. You can, however, impose your standards of excellence; insisting on the ultimate in professionalism only follows the contemporary view you seek to embrace.

It's true that some secretaries perceive women managers as more "demanding" than the traditional male boss. This can be a good sign. It sometimes means that, unhampered by stereotyping, a manager realizes a secretary is capable of more than typing. Going hand in hand with "demanding," woman bosses are sometimes called "picky." The *Working Woman* survey revealed that secretaries to women managers report more conflict than do those with male bosses over work not being done fast enough or work mistakes.

If you're considered demanding or picky, it may just mean your secretary has become accustomed to working for less-enlightened bosses who haven't expected that much from him or her in the past. As I've said before, many secretaries need enlightenment too. It may be fair to say that women bosses in general are more enlightened than men—perhaps because so many rose from secretarial ranks themselves and know what a secretary can do. And many women executives do have secretarial roots: according to a recent survey of 142 women executives in New York City, 37% had their start as secretaries; nearly half of the women managers responding to the *Working Woman* survey were former secretaries.

There is a danger, though, especially among those former secretaries, of being *too* demanding and picky in what is perhaps a conscious or unconscious hazing ritual. Insisting on high performance standards is one thing, giving your secretary the same hard time you may have experienced on your way up is quite another. As *Working Woman* advised in its survey report, "Just because you had to work for a so-and-so once doesn't mean *she* should have to."

I Deserve Respect, Don't I?

Secretaries observe that some women managers *demand* respect—presumably based on the position they have fought so hard to gain. To a secretary, position alone does not merit respect; it must be earned, and the way to earn it is to exhibit respect for your secretary. Remember, respect is a very sensitive issue for secretaries. It's the first test a manager must pass in order to win the loyalty of a secretary and the last chance he or she will get if that test is failed. This is, of course, true whether a manager is male or female.

Demanding respect can be the sure road to disaster, as Sally's story reflects. For 17 years, Sally was Executive Secretary to Jim, Executive Vice President of a large department of a *Fortune* 500 company. Five years prior to Jim's retirement, a woman was hired to be groomed for his position. Meredith had great credentials, and by Sally's own description, "had a lot of brains, but no smarts—she didn't know how to handle people on a one-to-one." Sally tells her story:

At first, Meredith was pleasant and cordial, but then she started to bring out a chip on her shoulder—she didn't like taking orders or being told what to do. After a period of time she started showing evidence of an uncontrollable temper. Then she also began to be insubordinate to Jim—he would ask her to do assignments and she would refuse to do them. It was an awkward position for him to be in. I started complaining to Jim to do something about her. To me, it was clear that Jim let her walk all over him because she was a woman in management, degreed, so therefore she was filling two quotas—hiring a woman, and hiring a degreed manager. Because she was a woman, he didn't make waves about her behavior. She was insubordinate—but he'd let it ride, gave her another chance, and she'd walk all over him.

Rather than asking me to do her work, she'd *insist* I do it. It was the way she asked—she demanded it be done—it was an automatic turnoff. And she demanded that I do her work *before* doing Jim's and, of course, my loyalty lies with him after 17 years. I wasn't going to let her push me around.

I had gone to Personnel a month or so before the big blow-up to tell them that tension was growing and that it would eventually explode between us and it did. Her uncontrollable temper came out one afternoon.

Something was bothering her—to this day I don't know what it was—something to do with a meeting she and Jim had earlier that day. She came out of her office, walked over to my desk and pushed all the files on the floor. She didn't say anything. Just did it. I said, "What is your problem?" To this day I regret not making her pick up every piece.

We were screaming at each other. She was saying that things had to be done for her. She said, "I demand respect." I said, "You'll get it when you earn it." Then Jim came out to see what the commotion was all about, and she started yelling at him. She did all the work and he got all the credit, she was getting fed up.

There was an investigation by the President's office. If I had started it, I probably would have been fired, but since Meredith started it she was just given a tap on the hand and told not to make waves.

Now things are different. She has Jim's job and I'm her assistant—no longer a secretary. Now she's a totally different person—because she's in charge, she doesn't have to take orders from anyone except the President. Most of the time I have free rein to do my job without supervision. There are times when we have differences of opinion, but it's not as tense as it was before.

New roles, different relationship—overall, a not-so-unique story that teaches many lessons.

First, Meredith made a fatal error in not recognizing that she, Meredith, was in effect an interloper within a team with a 17-year history. Not only did she command that her work get done *and* that Sally put Jim's aside to do it, but she demanded Sally's respect as well. It just doesn't work that way. Maybe Sally was right—Meredith had no "people sense." Common sense should dictate that the new kid on the block has to ease his or her way in to be accepted by the neighborhood.

In Meredith's defense, Sally really made no attempt to see things through Meredith's eyes. Meredith had a temper, yes, and there's no excuse for losing one's cool. But there was obviously something happening between Jim and Meredith. Maybe she *was* up against a boss who saw her as a quota filler. It certainly would have been frustrating to work hard, feeling the necessity to prove her worth, and have Jim in effect gloss over her contributions by presenting them as his own.

Speaking of Jim, his behavior might strike you as peculiar. What was he doing while Meredith and Sally were going at it? He was observing from the sidelines and probably just hoping that they would work it out between them.

Getting back to the women, Sally may have been more tolerant had she understood the situation from Meredith's perspective. To Sally, Meredith's behavior was astounding—"I don't understand what her problem was. She *had* Jim's job—she was hired specifically for it. It's not as if she were fighting 10 people to get it." It doesn't appear that Meredith made any attempt to communicate with Sally on a meaningful level.

It would have been interesting to see what would have happened if Meredith had tried to help Sally see things from her point of view. Would Sally's loyalty to Jim have stood in the way? Would woman-to-woman dynamics have ruled—and Sally refused to support Meredith just because she's a woman? It's not easy to predict. The fact remains, Meredith did not choose to make the attempt.

And what about those unspoken issues? Isn't it interesting that Sally doesn't seem to see anything wrong with viewing Meredith as a quota—in spite of the fact that Sally herself recognized that Meredith was "brilliant." Did unconscious rivalry move Sally to ignore Meredith's obvious ability? And how much of Sally's resentment had more to do with envy over her credentials and opportunity than her attitude?

When women work together, it can be complex. But let's get back to basics. The story provides an elementary lesson to all managers sharing a secretary whose first loyalty lies with another manager: ask nicely for your work to be completed, and you may be served. But a secretary may well consider it a favor, not your due.

I'm a Businesswoman First, Why Isn't She?

Women managers often find they must act like men in order to succeed. This means showing a concern for work above all, to the exclusion of home and family—at least outwardly. As one former secretary/then manager/now expectant mother reports:

> I left my job when the company was bought out. Although I was offered a position with the new headquarters office, I chose not to move to another city. I had it in the back of my mind that it might be a good time to start a family, but of course didn't give that as a reason. Now I really wonder what Marty [her former boss] and the rest of the people in the department are thinking about me when they hear through the grapevine that I'm expecting. I was always so "gung ho career"—if anyone mentioned babies, I'd worry aloud about what it would do to my career path. I realized it was an unwritten rule that I should say that, even if I didn't completely feel it, if I wanted to get ahead.
>
> I ran into trouble when I expected the same behavior from my secretary, who was pregnant during my last six months with the company. She was so openly pre-occupied with preparing for the baby and it bothered me that she didn't give 100% to her work. But then I realized that rule just doesn't exist among secretaries—because no matter how you look at it, it's still a female-dominated profession. It didn't seem fair, yet I understood where it came from, having been there myself.

Here's an area where women managers and secretaries often clash. A female secretary may expect a manager, as another woman, to be sympathetic to personal demands. Women managers, on the other hand, forced to suppress family concerns in order to fit in a male-dominated arena, may expect secretaries to do the same. So who's right? Are secretaries merely naive to the politics of career success? Or are women managers buying into male domination by trying to be something they're not? The answer to both questions may well be "yes," but that doesn't mean either point of view is right or wrong. It's just a reflection of the way it is. Until society works this one out, what's important is that manager and secretary come to terms on what they will expect of each other in their given circumstances.

MAKING IT WORK

We've discussed the potential traps that can impede the success of the woman manager/secretary or assistant relationship. We've also mentioned several advantages the woman boss can bring to the relationship. Let's elaborate on these advantages and put it all together.

It's been pointed out that many women bosses had their start in the secretarial ranks. If you're one of those, draw on that experience. The former secretary is aware of how a secretary can contribute and can be inclined to assign more than the usual "secretarial" types of tasks—a definite positive. The exception may be women who have a difficult time delegating, either because they view it as "dumping" on a secretary or because they fear losing a piece of their work. Remember—support staff often crave the opportunity for more responsibility—your guilt feelings are probably unfounded. As for feelings you must do it all yourself—remember what management means: getting things done through other people. You still get credit for work successfully performed under your supervision, and you get the added benefit of motivating your secretary at the same time.

Having been "in the trenches," so to speak, former secretaries may be more sensitive to the pet peeves of secretaries. For example, many secretaries observe that women bosses are less likely to require the performance of personal service types of tasks. *Working Woman*'s survey provided statistics to support this contention:

MALE BOSSES GET MORE PERSONAL SERVICE

When asked, "In your office, which of the following tasks are secretaries expected to perform?" secretaries' answers tend to differ according to whether they work for a man or a woman.*

	Secretaries with	
	Male Bosses	Female Bosses
Take dictation	74%	60%
Clean coffeepot	48	32
Sharpen pencils	46	41
Make personal arrangements for boss	40	29
Run personal errands for boss	39	37
Get boss's lunch	30	27
Balance boss's checkbook, pay his/her bills	14	6

*14% of secretaries surveyed have female bosses.
Reprinted with permission from *Working Woman* magazine. Copyright © 1986 by Working Woman, Inc.

Again, there's nothing wrong with personal service so long as a secretary knows from the start that it's a part of the job. The fact remains, however, that many secretaries appreciate letting go of that part of the job in the name of a contemporary view.

Secretaries report working for the woman boss has its advantages even if that boss was never a secretary. For one thing, many secretaries find women bosses to be more considerate and less likely to procrastinate or assign work at the last minute. And in spite of the possible differences among women in how they place their work/family/personal priorities, secretaries do report that women have a better understanding of a secretary's outside demands.

Here's a story that gives a view of how women managers can be successful. Janet has worked for not one, but two, women managers for three and a half years. She gives a glowing report:

> First of all, they are women, and smart as they are, they are a thousand times better than the men I have worked for. They're always fair and they treat me like a person. They have never ever missed an occasion, like Secretaries Day or my birthday. Once I was away for three days and they even gave me "Welcome Back" flowers on my return. They're so much more appreciative than any of the men I have worked for in past.
>
> It's my bosses as individuals, though—not all women.

There are some other women here who are equal to them in power, but I don't think I could ever work for them because of their attitude. I don't know these women, but from my observations, they seem bitchy—like they're power tripping—it's a kind of smugness. They're not friendly or nice, they never smile.

Susan and Maura are definitely exceptions because they're both such good people as individuals and because they're so intelligent. They know how to deal with people and gain loyalty. Some I attribute to their being women—the other part is just they're so smart.

The women part is the sensitivity, nurturing, things in common, just life and the things we like to do—playing sports—I have something in common with both of them so there are things we can talk about and feel comfortable with each other. It's an office friendship—I don't see them outside the office except when they take me out for different occasions, or when I work late, Maura drives me home because it's on her way and we talk—about work, about our lives.

It's really perfect—almost too perfect, because I have ambitions—I'd like to get into administration—but the only way I could advance is to leave, and since they're so good I don't have the motivation to leave. It's certainly not a bad thing, but you can get very comfortable.

It's obvious that these women managers have found just the right balance of mixing business and personal in the relationship. Perhaps because of this balance, there appear to be no undercurrents of rivalry among them—it would appear communication is open, honest and meaningful. And they've hit on a major key to success with secretaries—appreciation and recognition. Janet feels valuable and a part of the team. So much a part, she feels torn about leaving, although after three and a half years, some part of her feels it may be nearing time to move on.

It's good to hear that some of the socialized qualities of women—consideration, nurturing, sensitivity—can have a positive effect on the relationship. And, once again, it's pointed out that when it comes to secretaries working for women, success of the relationship depends on the individuals involved.

So, it all comes back to you. A woman manager must strive, like her male counterparts, to develop a successful relationship on a one-to-one basis with her secretary. Here's a checklist specifically for the woman manager.

A Checklist for the Woman Manager

1. Recognize how woman-to-woman dynamics may be influencing your relationship. Seek to understand your secretary's perspective of you and try to help your secretary accurately understand your situation—open and honest communication is crucial.
2. Build your secretary's self-confidence. Respect her expertise and allow her to take pride in her work. If she's content with a supportive role, so be it. If she seeks to follow in your footsteps, be her coach and mentor—you can only look the better for it.
3. Don't impose your values on your secretary. Reassure her that her value system is acceptable, so long as you both agree that when at work, work comes first. Set up standards and limitations that take into account the specifics of your personal realities. Come to a workable agreement and stick to it.
4. Work toward an appropriate personal/business balance with your secretary. Don't be overly friendly, nor overly aloof. Avoid being cast in non-work-related roles and keep from doing the same to your secretary.
5. Watch out for "trigger behaviors" to which your secretary or assistant may be particularly sensitive:
- Don't come on like gangbusters; let the relationship build on mutual respect at its own pace.
- Don't be overly apologetic about assigning mundane tasks. *Working Woman* advises: "It may work well to stifle your instinct to apologize at the outset and turn it into plentiful thanks once the chore is done."
- Don't patronize a secretary who doesn't share your obsession for climbing the corporate ladder. *Working Woman* calls this "careerist snobbery." As they aptly put it, "[Your secretary] can be loyal and willing to work as part of your team without wanting to make herself over in your image."

With awareness and conscious effort, a woman manager can not only build a successful, mutually beneficial relationship with a support professional, but even perhaps help to turn around what has too long been a "negative sisterhood" among women.

PLANNING FOR THE OFFICE OF THE FUTURE

This book has been designed to help today's manager survive the support staff crunch and take best advantage of the support staff/manager relationship. With the right approach, you can attract and hold the elusive high-caliber support professional in today's labor-short market and utilize your secretary's or assistant's talents to help you get ahead in your own career.

This book talks not only to the individual manager, but to companies and support professionals too. It has prescribed behaviors and action plans, and, most importantly, has shown a new way of thinking about the support staff role and function in today's business environment.

Rediscovering Support Staff as Valued Team Members

Forward-thinking companies will take steps to better integrate support staff into the corporate structure. Secretarial advisory committees and task forces can be created made up of managers, office support and human resource development staff to:

- Recommend company standards for support staff positions and develop or rewrite accurate job descriptions for individual support staff positions.

- Assign appropriate titles to positions rather than labeling all support staff "secretaries" or using broad categories that do not accurately reflect the function of individual secretaries.
- Create support staff compensation systems based on job content, position value and individual performance rather than tying salaries to the level of manager to whom the support person reports.
- Identify and restructure support staff career ladders to provide opportunities for advancement.
- Establish appropriate recognition programs for support staff contributions to organizational goals.
- Support and encourage support staff involvement in professional associations that provide for growth and development.
- Open communication channels to bridge the management/support staff gap and provide a forum for problem-solving among support staff and managers.
- Provide skill training and development opportunities for support professionals.

SUPPORT STAFF: A TICKET TO ENHANCED COMPETITIVENESS

Until recent years, a relatively small part, if even that, of an organization's training and development budget was invested in support staff since, it was commonly reasoned, support staff were not considered direct contributors to the bottom line. In today's information and service age, it has been observed that support staff are, in fact, the means by which a company's product—the brainpower of its staff—makes its way to the marketplace. It therefore follows that the company with the most effective support system will have an edge over its competitors.

The connection made between support staff and competitive advantage, many progressive companies are rethinking the value of investing in the development of support staff as fully functioning team members. Perhaps a company's most valuable hidden resource, support staff can be a key to enhanced productivity if their potential is maximized.

Training and development opportunities can build morale and enhance the motivation of workers who traditionally suffer from low self-esteem and feelings of powerlessness resulting from the "perception gap" between the stereotype and reality of today's support staff role. Traditionally overlooked, undervalued and underutilized, support staff are ripe and ready for transformation into fully contributing members of the organizational team.

DOWNSIZING AND THE "BABY BUST": INCREASED NEED AND A CHANGING WORKFORCE

The trend to eliminate what has been dubbed the "corpocracy" of American business—the corporate version of bureaucracy that many believe is a main reason for the decline of American competitiveness in world markets—means that organizations in all industries are pruning their staffs and emphasizing human resource development so that every employee in the human resource pool is fully utilized. Office support professionals must be included in this trend. Managers with outmoded attitudes may be roadblocks to progress—and may well find themselves left along the trail rather than among the pioneers in the company of the future.

The shrinking corporation and the growing emphasis on human resource development are two of three trends forecasted by John Naisbitt and Patricia Aburdeen in *Re-inventing the Corporation*. The third trend is the coming seller's market created by the "baby bust" generation. It is significant here because it magnifies the number one problem with support staff—the shortage of them.

Naisbitt and Aburdeen point out that during the 1970's, companies had the luxury of being choosy about whom they hired because of the baby boom and the increase in the number of women entering the workforce. During that decade, the number of people in the 18-to-24 age group—from which most corporations recruit their entry-level workers, including support staff—increased 22%. In the 1980's, that age group will decline by 15% and in 1990, there are 4.5 million fewer entry-level workers than in 1980, according to the U.S. Census Bureau. An article entitled "The Future of HRD," which appeared in the June 1989 issue of *Training & Development Journal*, reported that as the growth of the labor force slows from 2.9% a year in the 1970's to a projected 1% a year in the 1990's, the average age of workers is increasing while the number of younger workers is decreasing.

As overall availability of workers decreases, the profile of the workforce is also changing. Increasing numbers of women, minorities and adult students are preparing to enter or reenter the workforce. Meanwhile, we can expect that support staff roles will continue to expand and evolve rapidly.

Training can narrow the gap between educational levels and advancing skills requirements, allowing companies to hire from a broader, yet trainable pool. At the same time, a compensation package that includes training will attract better-educated, highly motivated candidates. Turnover may be reduced as studies have cited inadequate educational benefits and few opportunities for advancement as reasons for dissatisfaction among support staff workers. Support staff development programs, coupled with career pathing, will meet the needs of today's support professional who, we know, seeks career advancement, perhaps further reducing the cost of turnover.

ADVANCED TECHNOLOGY IN THE INFORMATION AGE: THE NEED FOR TRAINING AND DEVELOPMENT

Taking what we know and can predict about the office of the future, we can be reasonably certain that the role of support staff will continue to be central to the critical information management function of a company. Continuing advances in technology and an increased emphasis on access of information cast support staff in a pivotal role in the future workplace.

According to Paul Strassman, author of *Information Payoff—The Transformation of Work in the Electronic Age*, the future manager's ability to independently read, process, store and retrieve the information necessary to accomplish his or her work goals will be precluded by its sheer volume. Strassman had these words for secretaries attending Secretary Speakout® '87* on the topic of "Knowledge Management: Opportunity for the Secretary of the Future":

> In 1992 there will be 1.5 trillion pages of reading generated—24,600 pages for each information worker. If we don't deal with that, nobody will be able to understand what all of this information means. Nobody will be able to find the one page he wants. . . .
>
> When [executives] go to meetings, they have to go prepared . . . [they] cannot walk into negotiations any more and

---

*A trademark of Professional Secretaries International.

just play it by ear. It is becoming very important to have briefings about who called whom, who said what, what document recorded what, and who approved of what.

The business environment is becoming much more like library or legal environments which require enormous research and organizational skills.

Technical training and comprehensive development programs will be needed to prepare the support professional to meet a growing demand for highly skilled information managers. Important topics include:

TECHNICAL TRAINING

Word Processing and Computers
Business Writing, Editing and Proofreading
Customer Service and Selling
Time Management
Information Management and Networking
Accounting and Math
Budgets and Planning
Telephone Handling
Industry and Technical Terminology
Research

SKILL DEVELOPMENT

Communication and Conflict Resolution
Assertiveness and Negotiation
Business Etiquette and Professionalism
Certified Professional Secretary
Team-building
Decision-making and Problem-solving
Stress Management
Management Principles
Leadership
Delegation and Supervision
Risk-taking and Creative Thinking
Career Planning
Managing Change
Balancing Career and Family

THE OFFICE SUPPORT PROFESSION: CHALLENGE, VERSATILITY AND BALANCE FOR THE WORKER OF THE 1990'S

The road ahead promises increasing challenge and opportunity for the office support professional as roles continue to expand and evolve and support staff become increasingly critical to an organization's success. Multiple career paths, meaningful work, enhanced status and higher salaries await those who choose careers as office support professionals. Changing times also make careers in office support appealing.

The new decade brings with it a new set of values in our society. According to an article entitled "Corporate Caretaking" in the April 1990 issue of *Training & Development Journal*, 73% of women age 25 to 74 are now in the workforce and that percentage is expected to increase to 85% by the year 2000. Yet while women have established an intent to remain in the workforce, they are rejecting the superwoman myth and seeking ways to successfully combine work with a satisfying home life. Meanwhile, women's serious entry into the workforce has given men a chance to experience shared family roles, and, it seems, many enjoy this decidedly more active role.

As men and women alike seek more balance in their lives, perhaps the logical approach to work may shift from "go for the top" to finding meaningful, rewarding work. Realistically speaking, there just isn't room at the top for everyone, in any event. If downsizing trends continue to flatten pyramidal hierarchies, this will be an even more compelling fact of life in the future.

Support staff work close to the action, often right next to the center of power, without bearing the kind of responsibility that an executive must shoulder. The supporting role can be stimulating, meaningful and exciting while allowing a person to maintain a life outside the office. If support staff are drawn in as team members and afforded the same opportunities to contribute as other staff members, office support careers may become increasingly appealing to men and women who seek a balanced life.

As men and women struggle with the demands of juggling work and family, employers are recognizing the need to retain their top workers and looking for ways to create an environment that fosters satisfaction and productivity. A common solution is work schedule flexibility, to which support positions are particularly suited. Support positions have already proved adaptable to alternative work schedules, shared jobs and part-time scheduling.

And let's not forget that the office support profession is virtually the only profession that offers global mobility and adaptability. What industry or region *doesn't* use support staff?

Marketing the Support Profession

Intensive marketing efforts are required to educate people as to what secretarial careers have to offer—in general, and within specific industries and organizations—and to convince students and workers that office support careers are worth pursuing. It may well be worth your effort to get involved in such marketing efforts. Here's where you can turn for help.

The National Task Force on the Image of the Secretary was created in 1980 to bring together educators and the business community to find solutions to the growing support staff shortage. The Task Force is a coalition of associations and organizations, including the Association of Independent Colleges and Schools, the National Business Education Association, the American Vocational Association and Professional Secretaries International. Activities of the Task Force focus on making educators, career counselors and managers aware of the career opportunities available to secretaries and to emphasize the importance of the support professional to business. The Task Force theme: "Secretary: A Career of Distinction. BE ONE!" Its mission statement: "To enhance the image of the secretary by attracting qualified individuals to the secretarial profession and by promoting the career opportunities that exist in the field." See the Appendix for further details.

A New Management Perspective

Running American business lean and mean, moving toward an information and service economy, focusing on human rather than financial capital—these are all trends that can mean a bright future for the office support profession. To the organization with foresight, support staff can be the key to future success. Only the most progressive managers and companies will gain this competitive advantage. It's up to you. Will you survive and benefit from the secretarial crunch?

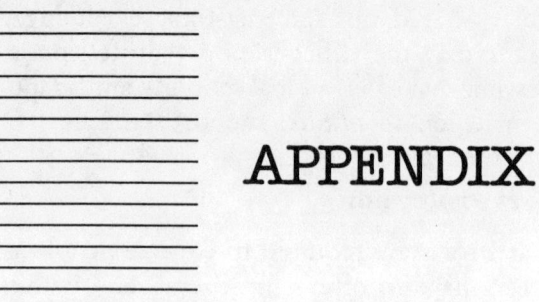

APPENDIX

Following are professional associations, organizations and other resources that can provide information and services or serve as a source of potential secretarial candidates.

PROFESSIONAL SECRETARIES INTERNATIONAL® (PSI)

Established in 1942, PSI is a nonprofit, nonunion, nonsectarian, worldwide association committed to the mission to effect increased productivity, career development and quality of work life within the office environment by providing opportunities for educational, personal and professional growth. PSI has 730 chapters throughout the United States, its territories, Puerto Rico and Canada, plus many international affiliates with members from all industries.

PSI offers many valuable programs and activities through its various departments.

Institute for Certifying Secretaries® (ICSR) offers two certification programs: the Office Proficiency Assessment and Certification® (OPAC®) examination tests entry-level competency; the *CPS®* (Certified Professional Secretary®) examination is for experienced secretaries.

Institute for Educating Secretaries® (IES®), oversees PSI's two student organizations: Future Secretaries Association® (FSA®), composed of high school students, and Collegiate Secretaries International® (CSI®), for postsecondary students.

PSI Research and Educational Foundation provides funds for projects that benefit secretaries, management and the educational field. The foundation coordinates and authorizes research, distributes findings and provides public instruction related to the secretarial profession.

PSI Office Opportunities Model Curriculum® *and PSI Post-Secondary Model Curriculum for Office Careers*® are available from PSI for secondary and postsecondary business education.

Establishment of corporate chapters, in industries such as health services, banking, communications, insurance, government and education.

Career path guidelines are being developed by PSI that include salary ranges, titles, education and training requirements, and job descriptions.

For information on PSI and its programs, contact:

Professional Secretaries International
10502 N.W. Ambassador Drive
P.O. Box 20404
Kansas City, MO 64195
(816) 891-6600

NATIONAL TASK FORCE ON THE IMAGE OF THE SECRETARY

Brochures, posters, buttons, stickers, a videotape and an annotated bibliography on the "Image of the Secretary" are available for promotion of the profession. You can obtain these and further information by writing or calling:

National Task Force on the Image of the Secretary
c/o AICS
One DuPont Circle, N.W., Suite 350
Washington, D.C. 20036
(202) 659-2460

OTHER ASSOCIATIONS THAT HAVE SECRETARIES AS MEMBERS

National Association of Legal Secretaries
2250 E. 73rd Street, Suite 550
Tulsa, OK 74136
(918) 493-3540

National Association of Rehabilitation Secretaries
c/o National Rehabilitation Association
633 South Washington Street
Alexandria, VA 22314
(703) 836-0850

National Association of Educational Office Personnel
7223 Lee Highway, Suite 301
Falls Church, VA 22046
(703) 533-0810

Association of Desk and Derrick Clubs
   (Petroleum Industry)
9920 East 42nd Street, #206
Tulsa, OK 74146

National Association of Secretarial Services
100 Second Avenue, S., Suite 604
St. Petersburg, FL 33701
(813) 823-3646

American Association of Medical Assistants, Inc.
20 North Wacker Drive
Suite 1575
Chicago, IL 60606
(312) 899-1500

National Association of Executive Secretaries
900 S. Washington Street, #G-13
Falls Church, VA 22046
(703) 237-8616

Society of Architectural Administrators
c/o Deborah Worth, President
HDR, Inc.
11225 S.E. Sixth Street
Building C, Suite 200
Bellevue, WA 98004
(206) 453-1523

Executive Women International
Spring Run Office Plaza
965 E. 4800 Street, Suite 1
Salt Lake City, UT 84117
(801) 263-3296

The National Association for Female Executives
127 W. 24th Street
New York, NY 10011
(212) 645-0770

NEWSLETTERS

Creative Secretary's Letter, published biweekly by Prentice Hall, Dept. PIOP, Englewood Cliffs, NJ 07632-9940.

From Nine to Five, published biweekly by Dartnell, 4660 Ravenswood Avenue, Chicago, IL 60640.

Networking: The Voice of Today's Office Professional, published quarterly by Federal Express Corporation, 2005 Corporate Avenue, Memphis, TN 38132.

The Office Professional, published monthly by Professional Training Associates, Inc., 212 Commerce Boulevard, Round Rock, TX 78664-2116.

P.S. for Professional Secretaries, published semimonthly by the Bureau of Business Practice, 24 Rope Ferry Road, Waterford, CT 06386.

MAGAZINES

The Secretary, published monthly by Professional Secretaries International, 10502 N.W. Ambassador Dr., P.O. Box 20404, Kansas City, MO 64195.

REPORT ON SECRETARIAL COMPENSATION

Secretarial Grading Practices: 1990 Update includes data on job evaluation plans, secretarial title options, exemption issues, union status, shorthand requirements, classification control, manager/secretary team transfers, software usage, recruitment and retention strategies, and alternative career path options. The complete report also includes a review of the literature, sample job description packages that can be tailored to organizations of varying sizes, key criteria for differentiating among secretarial levels and methods for selling both management and job incumbents on a job content evaluation system. The cost for this 64-page report is $195 (U.S.), prepaid including postage and handling and can be ordered from:

>N. E. Fried and Associates, Inc.
>5590 Dumfries Court West, Suite G
>Dublin, Ohio 43017
>(614) 766-9800

DIRECTORY OF SECRETARIAL AND SUPPORT STAFF RESOURCES, TRAINING PRODUCTS AND EXPERTS

The Secretarial/Clerical Trainers (CLASSE) Network of the American Society for Training and Development publishes an annual directory of products and services specifically designed for support staff. The cost for this directory is $12 for ASTD and $17 for non-ASTD members prepaid and can be ordered through:

>Secretarial/Clerical Trainers Network
>Susan Barenholtz
>CLASSE Directory
>29222 Lancaster #205
>Southfield, MI 48034

INDEX

absenteeism, 139
Aburdeen, Patricia, 155
administrative assistants, 53
administrative skills
    evaluating, 40–42
    in secretaries' duties, 69–72
advancements, informing applicants about, 44
advertisements, 52–55
    by employment agencies, 56
    personnel departments and, 51
    salaries in, 117
    telephone calls in response to, 62
Alfred (New York), State University of New York College of Technology at, 3–5
American Management Association, 123
appearance, at interviews, 60
appointments, responsibility for making, 91
appraisals of job performance, 137–40
appreciation, 120–21
    Professional Secretaries Week, 122–24
Arthritis Foundation, 123
assertiveness, 110–11
assigning responsibility and authority, 84–86
attitude problems, 4
authority, assigning, 84–86

"baby bust" generation, 155
behavior
    pet peeves, 131–32
    between secretaries and managers, 124–31
    of women managers, 143–49
benefits
    listed in advertisements, 52
    perquisites, 118–20
    relative importance of, 114, 115
billing, 94
bonuses, 119
Brennan, E. James, 115–17
business schools, 3

career paths
    relative importance of, 114, 115
    for secretaries, 16–17
    for support staff, 8
career planning, 140
career support staff, 43–45
Certified Personnel Consultants, 57
Certified Professional Secretary, 25n, 140
coffee klatch syndrome, 18–22, 108
college secretarial programs, 3
communications
    of conflict, 107–8
    of directions, 104
    feedback in, 104–6

communications *(continued)*
  grapevine connections in, 92–93
  during interviews, 60
  listening in, 106–7
  between management and support staff, 20–22
  of organizational goals, 101–2
  of priorities, 102–3
  problems in, 100–101, 109–12
  skills in, 40, 72
  support staff in information network, 23
  in teamwork, 97–99
  over telephone, of applicants, 62–63
compensation, 113, 115–18, 153–54
  perquisites as part of, 118–20
  relative importance of, 114–15
  for secretaries, report on, 164
compensatory time, 120
computers
  configurations of, 16
  in employment agencies, 56–57
  secretaries' skills with, 69
conflicts, 107–8
corporate culture, 34–35
critical incident method, 138

database management, 70
decision-making
  explanations for, 124–26
  secretaries' skills in, 78–79
  skills in, 40
  support staff left out of, 19–20
delegating responsibilities, 84–86
  in manager–support staff teamwork, 89–91
  to support staff, 94–95
  by women managers, 149
  in work styles, 30
dictating equipment, 38–39
dictation, 38
directions, communicating clearly, 104
discretion, during interviews, 61
discretionary skills
  evaluating, 40–42
  in performance appraisals, 138
  in secretaries' duties, 69–72
disorganization, 131
Duncan Group, 58

editing skills, 38, 72
employee evaluations, 137–40
employment agencies, 55–59

executive assistants, 53
  recruiting agencies for, 58
executive secretaries, 53
executive secretary search firms, 55, 58, 59
"exempt" job titles, 14–15, 133
experience, in recruitment, 45–46

family responsibilities, 29, 130, 148–49
favors, 129
feedback, 104–6
filing, 39, 70
flexibility, in working hours, 120
Fried, N. Elizabeth, 116, 133, 164
future, office of the, 153–59

gifts, 123–24
goals, 97
  communicating, 101–2
grapevines, 92–93

hours of work, 82–83
  compensatory time and, 120
  federal regulation of, 139

inconsistency, 131
industry
  mentioned in advertisements, 53–54
  salaries of secretaries tied to, 117
information
  advanced technology and, 156–57
  management of, 91–92
  skills in handling, 40
  support staff's access to, 23
information managers, 91–92
information retrieval, 70
information services, 2
innovation, support staff input, 19–21
intercoms, 127
internal recruitment, 49–50
interpersonal skills, 40, 72
interruptions, 131
interviews, 63–65
  appearance at, 60
  telephone, 62–63

job descriptions, 135–37
  in advertisements, 54
  for secretaries, 15–16
job-posting systems, 49
job satisfaction among secretaries, 114–15

job titles, 154
  in advertisements, 52–53
  "secretary" as, 8–9
  for support staff, 132–35
journals for secretaries, 120
judgment, of secretaries, 41

Katharine Gibbs School, 4–6

language skills, 5, 72
Lawley, Susan Marc, 89
legal issues
  "exempt" versus "nonexempt" job titles, 14–15
  in hours of work, 139
letters, dictating equipment used for, 38–39
listening, 106–7
loyalty
  of managers to support staff, 132
  of support staff to managers, 96–97
lunch hours, 19, 29, 82

magazines for secretaries, 120, 163
mail, handling of, 91–92
management
  explanations for decisions of, 124
  support staff not promoted into, 10
  support staff unity in face of, 18–19
management by objectives, 139–40
management skills, 78–79
managers
  behavior between secretaries and, 124–31
  blackballed by support staff, 21
  careers of secretaries tied to, 17
  communications between support staff and, 101–8
  determining support staff needs, 35–37
  dictating equipment used by, 38–39
  perceptions of secretaries' responsibilities, 68–69
  perceptions of support staff, 14–18
  performance appraisals by, 137–40
  problems communicating with support staff, 109–12
  raises negotiated by, 118
  responsibilities delegated by, 94–95
  secretaries' pet peeves about, 131–32
  secretaries salaries tied to, 116
  secretaries shared by, 87–88
  support staff loyalty to, 96–97
  teamwork between support staff and, 89–91, 97–99
  women as, 142–52
  work style of, 28–30
meetings
  informing support staff of purpose of, 102
  with support staff, 88
microforms, 39
motivation, 113

Naisbitt, John, 2, 155
National Association of Personnel Consultants, 57
National Secretaries Association, 122
National Secretaries Week, 122
National Task Force on the Image of the Secretary, 159, 161–62
newsletters for secretaries, 120, 163
nonassertiveness, 110
noncareer support staff, 43–45

objectives, 97
  communicating, 101–2
Occupational Outlook Handbook, 2
office of the future, 153–59
open-ended questions in recruitment, 62–63
ordering supplies, 85–86
organizational skills, 40
organizing, 80–82
overtime, 15, 29, 82, 139

pay, *see* compensation
perceptual skills, 40
perfectionists, 29–30
performance
  appraisals of, 137–40
  feedback on, 104–6
perquisites, 118–20
personal services, 149–50
personal telephone calls, 82
personality, 30–32
personnel departments, 50–52
  in performance appraisals, 140
pet peeves, 131–32
  of women managers, 148–49
planning
  for future office, 153–59
  secretaries' skills in, 79
prescreening applicants, 60–61
priorities, communicating, 102–3
privacy, 33–34, 126–27

168 • Index

private secretarial schools
  decline in enrollment in, 3
  job offers for graduates of, 4
  recruitment through, 59
problem-solving skills, 40, 78
procrastination, 30, 131
professional organizations
  importance of corporate support, 114
  sponsored memberships in, 119–20
Professional Secretaries Day, 120–22, 124
Professional Secretaries International (PSI), 25n, 114, 160–61
  associate members of, 57
  on communications problems, 100
  job titles collected by, 133–35
  Professional Secretaries Week, 122–23
  secretarial job description by, 135
  sponsored memberships in, 119–20
Professional Secretaries Week, 122–24
Professional Training Associates, 114
professionalism
  Professional Secretaries Week and, 122–24
  recognition of, 121
  in recruitment, 6
promises, 128–29
public relations
  skills in, 40, 71–72
  support staff in, 23–24
punctuality, 139

raises, 118
recognition, importance of, 114–15, 120–21
  Professional Secretaries Week and, 122–24
records management, 70
recruiting agencies, 55, 58, 59
recruitment
  advertisements in, 52–55
  career versus noncareer support staff, 43–45
  determining needs for, 35–37
  employment agencies for, 55–59
  evaluation of skills in, 37–42
  experience sought in, 45–46
  internal, 49–50
  listing needs for, 47–48
  making final choice in, 59–66
  personnel departments in, 50–52
  of secretaries, 27–28
  of secretaries' personality in, 30–32
  of secretaries' work environment, 32–34
  by temporary agencies, 4
references, 41
resumes, 55, 61–62
retainers, to recruiting agencies, 59
risk-taking, 109–10
role-playing, 111
routines, 86
rules, 82–84

salaries
  in advertisements, 53
  of secretaries, 115–18
  for support staff, 15
  see also compensation
Sawyer, Charles, 122
scheduling, 84–85
  priorities in, 102–3
secretarial schools
  decline in enrollment in, 3
  job offers for graduates of, 4
  recruitment through, 59
secretaries, 25–27
  administrative and discretionary skills, 40–42
  advertisements for, 52–55
  assigning responsibilities to, 84–86
  career paths for, 8
  career versus noncareer, 43–45
  choosing, 59–66
  communications problems faced by, 100–101
  compensation for, 115–18
  expanding roles of, 7
  experienced versus inexperienced, 45–46
  as information managers, 91–92
  internal recruitment of, 49–50
  as "invisible helping hand," 72–76
  job openings for, 2
  job satisfaction among, 114–15
  levels and titles of, 132–35
  management skills of, 78–79
  managers' behavior with, 124–31
  managers' perceptions of, 14–18
  obsolescence of term "secretary," 8–9
  performance appraisals of, 137–40
  perquisites for, 118–20
  pet peeves of, 131–32
  problems in communications between managers and, 109–12
  Professional Secretaries Week, 122–24

recruiting, 27–28
recruiting, agencies for, 55–59
recruiting, personality in, 30–32
recruiting, work environment in, 32–34
sharing, 87–88
skills of, 69–72
stereotyping of, 12–14
stigma attached to, 11–12
technical skills of, 37–40
training for, 95–96
to women managers, 142–52
work responsibilities of, 67–69
see also support staff
Secretary Speakouts, 123, 156
self-confidence, 110, 152
self-evaluations, 139
service industries, 2
sharing secretaries, 87–88
shorthand, 38
speedwriting, 38
spelling tests, 38
standards, 82–84
State University of New York College of Technology (Alfred, New York), 3–5
stereotypes of secretaries, 12–14, 26, 110–12, 140
   Professional Secretaries Week, 122
   by women managers, 144
Strassman, Paul, 156
strategies, corporate, 102
supplies, ordering, 85–86
support staff
   advertisements for, 52–55
   career paths for, 8
   career versus noncareer, 43–45
   choosing, 59–66
   communications between managers, 101–8
   compensation for, 115–18
   cost of turnover in, 10
   current role of, 79
   delegating responsibilities to, 94–95
   evaluating skills of, 37–42
   expanding roles of, 6–8
   experienced versus inexperienced, 45–46
   in information network, 23
   internal recruitment of, 49–50
   job descriptions for, 135–37
   levels and titles of, 132–35
   loyalty to managers of, 96–97
   management skills of, 78–79
   managers' perceptions of, 14–18
   managers' work style and, 28–30
   in office of the future, 153–59
   performance appraisals of, 137–40
   perquisites, for, 118–20
   preferred over "secretary," 9
   problems in communications between managers and, 109–12
   recognition and appreciation, 120–21
   shared, 87–88
   specialized skills of, 77–78
   stereotyping of, 12–14
   support groups among, 18–22
   teamwork between managers and, 89–91, 97–99
   temporary agencies for, 4
   training for, 95–96
   work environment of, 32–34
   see also secretaries

teamwork, between managers and support staff, 89–91, 97–99
   planning for, 153–55
   quiz on, 98–99
technical colleges, 3, 5
technical skills
   evaluating, 37–40
   in secretaries' duties, 69–72
technical training, 157
technology
   of document production, 7
   training for, 156–57
telephone
   appraisals of performance, 138
   calls made by secretaries for managers, 81–82
   personal calls, 82
   prescreening applicants by, 62–63
   responses to advertisements, 54–55
   skills, 39–40, 70–71
   style of answering, 81–82
temporary agencies, 4
testing
   by employment agencies, 58
   by personnel departments, 51
   of typing and spelling, 37–38
time management, 98
training
   for advanced technology, 156–57
   in assertiveness, 111
   for higher skills, 155–56
   relative importance of, 114

training *(continued)*
  for secretaries, 2
  for support staff, 95–96
travel arrangements, 85
trust, 96
turnover, 9–10, 155–56
typing, 69–70
typing tests, 37–38

wages, *see* compensation
Wisconsin Board of Vocational, Technical and Adult Education, 3
women
  changing aspirations of, 11
  as managers, 142–52
  shifts in social roles of, 5
  stereotyped roles of, 110–12
  wage discrimination against, 116
  in workforce, 158
women's movement, 11, 12, 110
Wood Secretarial School, 6
word processing, 69
work environment, 32–34
  corporate culture, 34–35
  privacy, 126–27
  roadblocks in, 97–98
work rules, 82–84
work styles, 28–30
  in interviews, 63–64
workforce
  demographics of, 155
  women in, 158

ABOUT THE AUTHOR

BETSY LAZARY is president of StepTakers, a training and consulting firm specializing in support staff effectiveness and development. Named Trainer of the Year by the Secretarial Trainers' Network of the American Society for Training and Development, she is also a past chapter president of Professional Secretaries International. A recognized authority on the changing role of the secretary, Ms. Lazary has made numerous television and radio appearances, presented at national conferences, is a frequent keynote speaker and has been widely published. She lives in Brewster, New York.

Additional copies of *Work with Me! How to Make the Most of Office Support Staff* may be ordered by sending a check for $9.95 (please add the following for postage and handling: $1.50 for the first copy, $.50 for each added copy) to:

> MasterMedia Limited
> 16 East 72nd Street
> New York, New York 10021
> (212) 260-5600
> (800) 334-8232

Betsy Lazary is available for speeches and workshops. Please contact MasterMedia's Speakers' Bureau for availability and fee arrangements. Call Tony Colao at (201) 359-1612.

Other MasterMedia Books

THE PREGNANCY AND MOTHERHOOD DIARY: Planning the First Year of Your Second Career, by Susan Schiffer Stautberg, is the first and only undated appointment diary that shows how to manage pregnancy and career. ($12.95 spiralbound)

CITIES OF OPPORTUNITY: Finding the Best Place to Work, Live and Prosper in the 1990's and Beyond, by Dr. John Tepper Marlin, explores the job and living options for the next decade and into the next century. This consumer guide and handbook, written by one of the world's experts on cities, selects and features forty-six American cities and metropolitan areas. ($24.95 cloth, $13.95 paper)

THE DOLLARS AND SENSE OF DIVORCE: The Financial Guide for Women, by Judith Briles, is the first book to combine practical tips on overcoming the legal hurdles and planning finances before, during and after divorce. ($10.95 paper)

OUT THE ORGANIZATION: How Fast Could You Find a New Job?, by Madeleine and Robert Swain, is written for the millions of Americans whose jobs are no longer safe, whose companies are not loyal and who face futures of uncertainty. It gives advice on finding a new job or starting your own business. ($17.95 cloth, $11.95 paper)

AGING PARENTS AND YOU: A Complete Handbook to Help You Help Your Elders Maintain a Healthy, Productive and Independent Life, by Eugenia Anderson-Ellis and Marsha Dryan, is a complete guide to providing care to aging relatives. It gives practical advice and resources to the adults who are helping their elders lead productive and independent lives. ($9.95 paper)

CRITICISM IN YOUR LIFE: How to Give It, How to Take It, How to Make It Work for You, by Dr. Deborah Bright, offers practical advice, in an upbeat, readable and realistic fashion, for turning criticism into control. Charts and diagrams guide the reader into managing criticism from bosses, spouses, children, friends, neighbors and in-laws. ($17.95 cloth, $9.95 paper)

BEYOND SUCCESS: How Volunteer Service Can Help You Begin Making a Life Instead of Just a Living, by John F. Raynolds III and Eleanor Raynolds, C.B.E., is a unique how-to book targeted to business and professional people considering volunteer work, senior citizens who wish to fill leisure time meaningfully and students trying out various career options. The book is filled with interviews with celebrities, CEOs and average citizens who talk about the benefits of service work. ($19.95 cloth, $9.95 paper)

MANAGING IT ALL: Time-Saving Ideas for Career, Family, Relationships and Self, by Beverly Benz Treuille and Susan Schiffer Stautberg, is written for women who are juggling careers and families. Over two hundred career women (ranging from a TV anchorwoman to an investment banker) were interviewed. The book contains many humorous anecdotes on saving time and improving the quality of life for self and family. ($9.95 paper)

REAL LIFE 101: (Almost) Surviving Your First Year Out of College, by Susan Kleinman, supplies welcome advice to those facing "real life" for the first time, focusing on work, money, health and how to deal with freedom and responsibility. ($9.95 paper)

YOUR HEALTHY BODY, YOUR HEALTHY LIFE: How to Take Control of Your Medical Destiny, by Donald B. Louria, M.D., provides precise advice and strategies that will help you to live a long and healthy life. Learn also about nutrition, exercise, vitamins and medication, as well as how to control risk factors for major diseases. ($12.95 paper)

THE CONFIDENCE FACTOR: How Self-Esteem Can Change Your Life, by Judith Briles, is based on a nationwide survey of six thousand men and women. Briles explores why women so often feel a lack of self-confidence and have a poor opinion of themselves. She offers step-by-step advice on becoming the person you want to be. ($18.95 cloth)

THE SOLUTION TO POLLUTION: 101 Things You Can Do to Clean Up Your Environment, by Laurence Sombke, offers step-by-step techniques on how to conserve more energy, start a recycling center, choose biodegradable products and how to proceed with individual environmental cleanup projects. ($7.95 paper)

TAKING CONTROL OF YOUR LIFE: The Secrets of Successful Enterprising Women, by Gail Blanke and Kathleen Walas, is based on the authors' professional experience with Avon Products' Women of Enterprise Awards, given each year to outstanding women entrepreneurs. The authors offer a specific plan to help you gain control over your life and include business tips and quizzes as well as beauty and lifestyle information. ($17.95 cloth)

POWER PARTNERS: How Two-Career Couples Can Play to Win, by Jane Hershey Cuozzo and S. Diane Graham, describes how two-career couples can learn the difference between competing with a spouse and becoming a supportive Power Partner. ($19.95 cloth)